Kate Vogt has crafted a book of great beauty and wisdom to remind us of our essential nature and our connection to all of life. She invites us to reclaim our sensual selves through play, touch, sound, movement, and breath. Thoughtfully chosen poems are springboards for her evocative storytelling, followed by a variety of meditative exercises that bring us back into relationship with all of life. Her writing illuminates the deep yet often ignored healing power embedded in communing directly with animals, sky, water, plants, and aspects of ourselves. It's easier than ever for 21st century humans to overlook or lose sight of what's true and essential. These grace-filled pages will call you back again and again when you need to remember.

> —Sharon Rosen
> Author, *Crazy World, Peaceful Heart*
> Healer and Coach

Kate's beautiful lyrical expressions of the Infinite draws one into the mystic pools of wisdom through the timeless voices of sages, mystics and poets.

> —Shambhavi Chopra
> Author, *Yogini: Unfolding the Goddess Within*
> and others.
> Educator, The American Vedic Institute

OUR INHERITED WISDOM

OUR INHERITED WISDOM
54 INSPIRATIONS FROM NATURE AND POETRY

Kate Vogt

PLAIN SPOKEN PUBLICATIONS

Our Inherited Wisdom
Copyright © 2020 by Kate Vogt
All rights reserved. No part of this publication may be reproduced, distributed, or transmitted in any form or by any means, including photocopying, recording, or other electronic or mechanical methods, without the prior written permission of the author, except in the case of brief quotations embodied in critical reviews and certain other noncommercial uses permitted by copyright law.

Published by: Plain Spoken Publications, Mill Valley, CA

ISBN: 978-1-7331819-2-1

- Religion & Spirituality - Inspirational
- Human Ecology - Religious Aspects
- Poetry – Inspirational & Mysticism

Edited by: wordsbylj.com
Cover Photo: GettyImages
Book Design: BookAlchemist.net

With loving appreciation to

Jay Rosner
Robert E. Vogt and Virginia Vogt

TABLE OF CONTENTS

Introduction	1
Divine Presence in All	
Plants and Trees	7
Insects, Birds, Reptiles, and Animals	43
Oceans, Rain, Rivers, and Tears	93
Divine Awareness and Mind	
Interconnectedness	125
Senses of Sight, Sound, and Touch	157
Inner Attitudes	189
Divine Freedom	
Sky and Light	233
Pause, Stillness, and Solitude	277
Love	313
Sources, Credits, and Permissions	344
Acknowledgments	348
Index	
Poet Index	349
Reflections and Practices Index	350
About the Author	355

INTRODUCTION

To see a World in a Grain of Sand
And a Heaven in a Wild Flower,
Hold Infinity in the palm of your hand
And Eternity in an hour.
—William Blake

My older sister Gail and I slipped out the back door. We were off for an early summer adventure, which would only reveal itself once we were outside. Since neither of us knew what we would tell our mother if she asked us where we were going, it seemed best to close the back door quietly.

The haystack beckoned, so we headed in that direction. In the morning light, it looked like a golden mountain rising up from the otherwise flat horizon. We knew that mother was not particularly fond of our climbing on the bales of hay, but our sense of exploration had already taken hold. No warnings about possibly encountering snakes or falling bales of hay could deter us.

On top of the haystack, we peered out over the expanse of land and sky. Even at ages seven and four, we knew that the outdoors was as much our home as our parents' house was. In fact, the boundary between the two was blurred. If we had read William Blake's words "to see a world in a grain of sand," we would have understood them. For us, the entire world was

OUR INHERITED WISDOM

in every straw of wheat, clump of dirt, mockingbird's song, or wisp of cloud.

Our family wheat farm was a half-century old. As members of the next generation, Gail and I had absorbed the wisdom of our elders. Just in the way they had learned from prior generations, life did not begin and end with humans. We were not superior to the rest of life. For example, insects were more powerful than we were. Overnight, they could consume not only the crops representing the family livelihood and months of work, but the food supply of grain for thousands of humans and animals. The microbes in the soil and the grace of moisture—snows and rains—were as essential as our father's work to an abundant harvest.

From our vantage point at the top of the bales of hay, there was a visceral sense of William Blake's insight about holding "infinity in the palm of your hand." We were perched far enough above the usual markers of space, e.g., the cows, and the fences around the pastures, so that any fears that we were supposed to have were absorbed in the immensity around us. Was it awe that we felt? Perhaps it was more that we were infused with a visceral understanding about reality. Timeless truths took root in the depths of our souls in a way that forever tethered us to the Infinite's living presence in every particle of life.

I used to imagine that if you kept walking, in any direction, you'd eventually come back to the same spot. My child's mind didn't consider that there were oceans and other hindrances to walking around the planet, so my dream was purely an imaginary journey. Yet, I had an intuitive under-

INTRODUCTION

standing that the tip of our haystack was as much home as anywhere. Up and down, heaven and earth, east and west, north and south all meet inside of our eternal home—our collective heart, held by infinite love.

As life has gone on, Gail and I have continued our explorations of life and the world. She has done so through books, and the capacity to delve into any topic of her choice. I have lived abroad and circumnavigated the globe. She has logged pages, while I have logged distances, and yet we have both tested how far afield we could wander and still find our way back to the inner gems of truth.

I believe that every human being has enduring wisdom tucked into his or her heart. The word "wisdom," for me, refers to the divine intelligence in all life. If there is anything that could bring eternal laughter, it is the discovery that if we go in search of this wisdom, we won't find it. When we stop searching, there it is—a pervasive, wordless knowingness. It is our planetary inheritance, yet it is so ordinary that we continue searching for it.

Fortunately, wisdom has not abandoned us. Even if we are unaware that its richness is everywhere, it is written in the sayings of our ancestors, the words of sacred poets, and in the plains, mountains, oceans, flowers, and trees. These are so accessible that we have become immune to their profound and lasting message to wake up and, literally, smell the roses.

Nature is like a conductor, drawing out and fine-tuning the notes written in our souls. Again and again, nature invites us to discover new insights, and opens us to shift our perspectives and attitudes. In our modern lives, we need nature

OUR INHERITED WISDOM

to draw the sacred notes out of our hearts and encourage us to re-harmonize with the divine song. Somehow, we have gotten temporarily sidetracked and are simply clanging along, although out of sync with eternal rhythms.

Every sunrise and sunset, starry night, full moon, rainbow, and fragrance are cues for us to remember we are part of this song. The most ancient wisdom is built upon keen observation, kinship, and reverence for elemental sustenance and the cycles of life. Universal principles such as compassion, love, authenticity, and harmlessness arise from beautifully harmonizing earthly and heavenly realms. As humans, we are given natural tools—eyes, mouths, ears, hands, and feet—to live as graceful, lyrical expressions of the Infinite.

Wise sages, saints, elders, and poets such as William Blake are in sync with the divine song. These discerning humans inspire us to re-attune our lives not only for our benefit but for the planet and all living species, including humanity. Nature and poetry open us to a remembrance of that which can never truly be forgotten. Our hearts might have become paved over like the surfaces of the planet and our minds might have been excavated like the jewels of the earth, but our souls will eternally long for uniting with the expanse of our immortal home.

As humans, we have the unique capacity to choose. In the 1700s, Swedish botanist Carl Linnaeus classified humans as "*homo sapiens,*" which comes from the Latin homõ ("human being") + sapiēnes ("wise, sensible, judicious"). This classification is an apt reminder to choose what our elders and ancestors knew—that the riches of life are hidden within the

INTRODUCTION

seemingly mundane. In this collection, I invite us to find our way home through the timeless voices of nature and poets.

Each reflection touches upon multiple realms of our existence as a way to stir inspiration within all parts of us. All of life is integrated and interconnected. We know this intellectually, but most of our learning takes place by categorizing and separating nature, body, mind, soul, as well as by outer results from our actions. This separatist experience of life is more common in the mainstream West, in part because of the philosophical influences of the Enlightenment on Western thought. Older rural communities and those who have worked closely with the elements have nurtured the universal, holistic perspective that is at the very heart of enduring ancient philosophy and wisdom.

There are 54 reflections; 54 is half of 108. The sacred number 108 carries a reference to our earthly and heavenly existence, in that the distance between our planet and the sun is 108 times the diameter of the sun. Symbolically, the sun is the eternal light of the Infinite. Astrologically, 108 represents the product of nine planets traveling through twelve signs. In mathematics, 108 is the product of the powers of 1, 2, and 3. The number 108 represents the Divine (1), emptiness (0), and infinity (8). Also, there are 108 beads in a sacred mala used in meditation in Eastern traditions.

Two cycles around a half-mala of 54 makes a full round. I invite you to make two rounds through this collection. On the first round, you may choose to simply read and experience. I suggest you spread out the second round over time. For example, you could read one reflection per week for a year,

OUR INHERITED WISDOM

with a bonus of two extra. The extra time would allow you to absorb and reflect on your own insights. It would also give you space to notice any shifts in your perspective. Each reflection offers doorways for you to revive your latent memories of belonging to and being attuned with the universe and your divine self.

My wish for everyone is that we once again synchronize our lives with timeless rhythms. If we are lucky enough to have the basic life comforts, such as food, housing, clothing, and basic physical and mental health, then we have the opportunity to be pioneers in this revival. As humans, we are a remarkable species, and I feel that with a little inspiration and discipline, we can tap into the depths of our potential to be wise and to live wisely.

May this collection inspire you "To see a World in a Grain of Sand, And a Heaven in a Wild Flower, Hold Infinity in the palm of your hand, and Eternity in an hour." I hope it strengthens your awareness and reverence for the sacredness of everyday moments. There is blank space at the end of each practice for your use.

Divine Presence in All
PLANTS AND TREES

DAFFODIL

> Dear God, please reveal to us
> your sublime
> beauty
>
> that is everywhere, everywhere, everywhere
>
> so that we will never again
> feel frightened.
>
> St. Francis of Assisi
> *Trans. by Daniel Ladinsky*

A loud siren was booming throughout our neighborhood. I was inside the house, putting clothes into the washing machine, but the sound fulfilled its purpose. As with most people who suddenly hear an alarm, my mind immediately shifted into high alert and sifted through the possibilities for its activation. Even though my husband and I live in an area prone to earthquakes and fires, I quickly dismissed either of those options, as there had been no ground shaking, and rain was pouring down. The neighborhood dogs began to howl. Then I remembered that a prescheduled test of our town's firehouse siren had been announced some days ago.

While it is an absolute necessity that we alert one another to impending danger—especially with the preponderance of natural disasters—I wonder what our world would be like if humans had invented "sublime beauty" alerts. If we had

OUR INHERITED WISDOM

regular sirens for every stunning natural occurrence, we'd be enveloped in constant awe of everything that sustains us.

Instead, we have used our ingenuity for threat alerts. Not the necessary ones like my neighborhood firehouse alarm, but a stream of promises to soothe every fear—be better looking, more productive, healthier, richer, more balanced, calmer, or happier. The modern commercial space subtly taps into our woes and wraps us into the comfort of their brand's product, app, or service. As a result, our lifestyles and habits rarely bring us in direct touch with nature. Our food is pre-packaged, our outdoor exercise requires equipment, our contemplation relies on apps.

Somehow, humanity has allowed itself to become enamored with cleverness—forgetting that homo sapiens refers to "wise human," not "clever human." Other species sing praises to the co-existence of all of life in an abundance of glorious shapes, forms, sounds, and fragrances. There are upheavals and invasiveness in other species, but we are unique in our trail of efforts to conquer, outsmart, and ignore the sacredness of all of life. We need the prayer of St. Francis of Assisi more than ever to bring us back in sync with one another, the planet, the divine, and ourselves.

The daffodil is where I choose to begin the re-righting of my human perspective, from a separatist to a holistic view. It is among the first spring blooms and is lauded around the world as a messenger of renewal and abundance. Its trumpet-shaped crown is an uplifting announcement of the unfolding of new energy and hope. It inspires us to tune into the wise messages that nature has to share.

DAFFODIL

PRACTICE

This practice supports appreciation of your everyday surroundings.

Prepare—
- This practice involves both being seated and standing. Choose a place that has minimal distractions.
- Remove your shoes and socks. Begin seated, with a gentle lift through the spine. If in a chair, place both feet on the floor.
- Look around the room, listen to the sounds, feel the air and the texture of your clothing on your skin. Do this as though you are looking at, listening to, and being with cherished friends.
- Place one palm on your heart and then the other on top. Breathe a few breaths. Relax through your palms, jaw, eyes, shoulders and torso.
- Release your hands to your thighs.
    - Breathe free and easy. Breathing, say to yourself, "I am in the midst of friends. The earth is supporting me, the breath is nourishing me, the space around me is enfolding me with love."

Practice—
- Stand. Remember, you are in the midst of friends who support, nourish, and enfold you in love.
- Slowly begin to walk around the room. Let each step be a gesture of your respect for the floor. If it is wooden, acknowledge the trees that were the source of the wood. If concrete, acknowledge the riverbeds and water that

OUR INHERITED WISDOM

formed the rocks and sand for the concrete. Acknowledge the workers and their hands that built the floor.
- Keep a gentle breath. After couple dozen steps, pause. (No worries about counting the exact number of steps. An approximate amount is fine.)
- Walk for another dozen or so steps. Acknowledge the walls, the ceiling, and their sources. Acknowledge the air and the trees that cleanse the air. Pause.
- Stand by your chair. Acknowledge the source of all life. Acknowledge God, or whatever you consider to be most supreme. Imagine you are filled with love and kindness.

Transition Back into Your Day—
- Seated, place both of your feet on the floor. Relax your palms in your lap. Allow your eyes to close, or to be gently open with a soft gaze. Breathe.
- After a few moments, return to your day.

DAFFODIL

A LEAF

> For everything there is a season,
> a time for every matter under heaven:
> a time to be born, and a time to die…
>
> Book Of Ecclesiastes 3:1-2

As I opened the front door to go on an early morning walk, a leaf floated onto the doorstep. It was heart-shaped and golden in color. I'd swept away a basketful of leaves the day before. The weather had been windy, and now it was calm, with no detectable breeze.

The fallen leaf reminded me of the ebb and flow of life. Solstice was approaching. It marked the onset of winter here in the Northern hemisphere. On the other side of the globe, spring would slide into summer. Everywhere there was renewal and release, darkness and light, birth and death.

The leaf, which had been a bud a few months ago, was also in transition. On the tree, it had had many roles. Primarily, along with other leaves, it provided nourishment for the tree. The chlorophyll, which is a special plant chemical, absorbs and converts the light of the sun into useable sugars and starches that fuel the tree's growth and stability.

If it could have told me its life story, I imagine that the leaf would have said that it began its journey as a minuscule rise on a branch. After it had sprouted, using the energy from the prior generation of leaves, it unfurled and became part of a new community of leaves. Together, they had not only fed the tree, but also helped provide protection and a home for numerous birds, squirrels, and insects. They weathered a drought and seamlessly worked together to produce oxygen and create shade for the world.

Once the days shortened, the leaf pigment changed. The canopy of green slowly shifted to the hues of the sun. At the same time, there had been an inner chemical transformation. Not only had the chlorophyll given way to carotenoid to create a beautiful golden color, but also the tree's cells were ready to release each leaf to the earth. Clinging to the tree wasn't an option. The leaf's next purpose was to create a layer to help the ground absorb water. Now, as it decomposes, the leaf will provide nutrients for the soil, so that a new generation can flourish.

I gently picked up the leaf and moved it to an uncultivated area along the street. There, it could continue its life journey undisturbed by rakes, brooms, or mechanized leaf blowers. I felt an appreciation toward this leaf. After all, it reminded me of the sacredness of life.

Prophets, sages and saints often point to the flowers, trees, seasons, and other parts of nature as ways to prompt our deep memory of eternal wisdom. A leaf signifies truth. The sun and sunlight are symbolic of divine light and love. Many ancient religions view all of life as leaves on a universal tree. On the surface, the leaf on my doorstep seems insignificant. It is one of trillions of leaves. Yet its story reveals the richness of a life that simply receives and is a conduit for light. That alone inspires me to adopt a light-hearted motto, "leaf it."

A LEAF

PRACTICE

This practice offers a personal connection with a leaf.

Prepare—
- Find a fallen leaf from a deciduous tree and gently pick it up. If you are not near trees, then simply imagining a leaf is fine.
- With the leaf lightly held in one hand, find a comfortable seated position. You may choose where you sit, e.g., inside or outside. Wherever you are, allow your spine to be upright, with its natural curvatures. If you are in a chair, place the soles of both feet on the ground.
  - Take a few easy breaths. Allow your lower abdomen to slowly expand on each inhale and to release on the "out" breath.
    - Your hands can be resting with palms open, either on your thighs, or on top of one another.
    - Relax any tension in your hands, jaw, back of your eyes, and base of your skull
- Gently close your eyes, or keep them in a soft gaze.

Practice—
- Without actively looking or touching, just become aware of the leaf.
  - Notice its lightness and texture. Feel its weight in the palm of your hand.
  - Continue your reflection on the leaf, without analyzing or forcing. Just imagine you are holding

OUR INHERITED WISDOM

something precious in your hand and that you let its richness and beauty soak into your awareness.
- If your mind is too active, try gently guiding it toward appreciating the leaf and its story. For example, appreciate the life of the leaf being fueled by a prior generation of leaves, and then being the nourishment for the next. Or, appreciate its ability to be steadily tethered to the tree during the intensity of wind blowing, and rainstorms.
- As your sit here, allow your breath to be smooth and easy. Continually release the tension in your palms, shoulders, face, neck, and behind your eyes.

○ Stay with this first part of the practice if your mind is distracted. If you feel you have been able to let go and just be present, then allow yourself to shift your awareness to your heart center.

○ Imagine your heart is like a leaf, free of human fears and worries and attachments.
- Allow the tension around your heart center to release.
- Imagine there is only lightness and expansiveness, without a tangible beginning or end. Remember, for this moment, you are a leaf free of human fears, worries, and attachments.
- Continue with a smooth, easy, and calm breath.
- Stay here for as long as you are comfortable.

A LEAF

Transition Back into Your Day—
- Still seated, gently open your eyes, if they were closed. With a soft gaze, notice the earthly light around you. Gently smile.
- When you are ready, return to your day. (If you picked up a leaf, eventually return it the earth.)

PINE TREE

Sitting over words
very late I have heard a kind of whispered sighing
not far
like a night wind in pines or like the sea in the dark
the echo of everything that has ever
been spoken
still spinning its one syllable
between the earth and silence

W.S. Merwin

The sky was a deep blue, with a light glow along the horizon. It was quiet, and the only discernible movements were a hawk soaring along invisible currents and a few butterflies and dragonflies. As I stood enveloped in this peaceful hillside, the hawk swooped close overhead. I paused momentarily in fear and then realized that the hawk's interruption had inspired me to sit down. There was a sweet aroma filling the air; I had settled near a large pine tree.

The tree had a sturdy trunk that disappeared into the rocky surface of the hill and into the tree's bundle of needles and cones. Atop the tree, one small branch reached toward the blueness of the sky. As I sat there, it seemed as though the tree had gathered me into its genus *pinus* world. The tree's ancestors had been growing up to 300 million years ago, far earlier than any of the flowering plant species. Humans are estimated to have been around for 6 million years. No wonder I felt an incredible sense of timeless peace and calm in the presence of this magnificent tree.

Pines grow throughout the northern hemisphere, and are beloved in many Native American and First Nation, Asian, Northern African, and European cultures. To many, pines are considered sacred, symbolizing some of the deepest lessons in life. Pines offer sustenance and protection to many species, while keeping a finely-tuned inner balance, from crown to roots. The human pineal gland, which is important to our biorhythms, resembles and is named after the nutritious pine nut. In Eastern traditions, the pineal gland is the seat of pure understanding and light.

The symbolism for the pine is extensive. Among its more than 100 species, the *Pinus longaeva* (bristlecone) can live up to 4,000 years. So, two of the most common symbolic references for the pine are longevity and eternity. Its pyramidal shape and high flammability link the pine to the secrets of fire and light. The spiral nature of its cones represents renewal and enlightenment. The span of the single stem signifies adeptness in all realms, and can serve as an antenna for divine grace. Its stability reminds us of everlasting wisdom, honor, virtue, and strength. Its many medicinal and functional uses expand its symbolism to humility, generosity, purification, prosperity, and health. Its peaceful presence offers a release from fear and stress, and a discovery of inner joy.

Through such grandeur, the pine encompasses all of life. Focusing on the words from the poem Pine Tree by W.S.

PINE TREE

Merwin, I maintain that the pine brilliantly synthesizes "all that has ever been spoken," leaving me with the single syllable of *aaah*.

PRACTICE

This practice invites a sense of timeless harmony.

Prepare—
- If at home, sit in a quiet place. Silence any potential distractions, such as your phone.
- Rotate your wrists in circles, a few times in both directions.
- Curl your fingers softly in toward your palm. Then stretch your fingers.
- Touch the tip of your thumb with tip of each finger.

Practice—
- Breathe.
  - Exhale smoothly, quietly and evenly through the nose. If your breath is congested or short, purse your lips and breathe out—as though trying to whistle.
    - As you exhale, stretch out your fingers and palms.
    - With each exhalation, imagine you are releasing your worries and a layer of stress through your fingertips.

OUR INHERITED WISDOM

- Inhale smoothly, quietly, and evenly through your nose.
  - As you breathe in, *slowly* fold your thumbs in toward your palm, i.e., right thumb toward right palm and left thumb to left palm. As you fold your thumbs inward, *lightly* fold your fingers over your thumb, i.e., right fingers over right thumb and v.v.
  - Imagine that as you gather your fingers together, you are drawing in pure light and love into every cell of your body.
  - If you are comfortable with the single syllable sound "Om," you may wish to instead imagine that you are drawing "Om" into every cell. Alternatively, you may wish to use *aaah*.
- Repeat the in- and out-breath and associated hand movement 6 to 12 times.

Transition Back Into Your Day—
- Sit for as long as you have time and are comfortable.
  - Allow your hands to rest in your lap.
  - Gently close your eyelids, or leave your eyes open in a soft gaze.
  - Relax your tongue, neck, throat, and the tops of your shoulders.
  - Notice the gentle rhythmic movement associated with your breath as it comes in and goes out.
- When you feel complete, return to your day.

PINE TREE

REEDS

All day and night, music,
a quiet, bright
reedsong. If it
fades, we fade.

Rumi
Trans. by John Moyne and Coleman Barks

As I walked on the path toward the sea, I felt more and more peaceful. The roadway sounds had dropped away, and the surface beneath my feet was softening. The trail meandered along a hillside covered with grasses of different colors and varieties. Birds were making their way to the lower side of the slope, which was filled with reed beds.

A local ecologist had recently written that reeds are important to the life of the landscape. Their rhizomes stabilize the sediment in marshy areas, and their stalks help protect the shore. In addition to structural support, they are a food plant for some species. They also improve the conditions for healthy microbial functions, regulate pollution control, and help support healthy water and environment. Large reeds, such as those along the Nile, can grow two or more meters high.

The reed connects us to our human story. Throughout the world, reeds have provided for our earthly necessities, e.g., food, bedding, containers, medicine, and instruments. Our

OUR INHERITED WISDOM

human heart and spine are like the reed in their flexibility and centrality to overall vitality. When healthy, they all quietly cleanse, nourish, support, and protect overall harmony and balance, and become conduits to knowing our immortal nature.

When transformed into a flute, the reed forms one of the most ancient and mystical musical instruments. The pains and sorrows of our life experiences are said to be the holes in the flute. And, when the flute speaks, it wails of being severed from the reed bed and sings of its deepest longing to return to its origin. The voice of the flute arises from the breath of the divine playing the reedsong through the musician's breath. Sincere listeners can hear the reed's secret song, melt any residual sense of separateness, and merge into the embrace of eternal divine love.

It is no wonder that I felt more peaceful as I neared the open ocean. The reeds were calling me home. In the coming weeks, in awareness of the reeds' message, I will be more attentive to caring for this precious embodiment as being integral to the well-being of all. I will particularly be attentive to the use of my voice, since, like the reed flute, sound is an expression of the breath, which is itself a divine gift.

REEDS

PRACTICE

This practice supports awareness of the reedsong of divine love.

Prepare—
- Turn off nearby electronic devices and remove your watch.
- Find a comfortable seated position.
    - If you are in a chair, please have both of your feet on the floor.
        - Notice the surface(s) beneath you and effortlessly balance your weight between the left and right sides.
    - As you settle down toward the earth, allow your spine and the crown of your head to gently lengthen upward.

Practice—
- Breathe a few comfortable and easy breaths.
- Imagine you are seated on the earth, surrounded by reeds. Beneath the surface, the reeds have a wide circle of roots.
    - Imagine that those roots represent eternal love. You are seated in the center of eternal love.
    - Imagine that each root is expanding outward, expanding love to an ever-widening circle. You are supported by love.
    - Imagine that each root is sprouting love. You are enfolded in love.

OUR INHERITED WISDOM

- Breathe. With each breath, remember:
  - You are held by love.
  - You are supported by love.
  - You are enfolded in love.
  - You are love.
  - All is love.

Transition Back into Your Day—
- Sit quietly for several moments.
- When you are ready, return to your day.

REEDS

SUNFLOWER

God, whose love and joy
        are present everywhere,
can't come to visit you
        unless you aren't there.

Angelus Silesius

The vendors were packing up. I had arrived just before closing at the local farmers' market, with the hope that it wasn't too late to buy some vegetables. Luckily there were still some bundles of chard, arugula and kale. Alongside the greens were sparks of the red, orange and green of the colorful radishes, carrots, and beets.

    I got sidetracked with a glimpse of yellow further down the aisle. If a heart can smile, mine did when I saw the source of the golden hue that had lured me in that direction. Sunflowers! These plants grow in abundance where I was raised, and are forever emblematic of home anchoring me on my life's journey.

    Sunflowers are hardy, and have long been part of human history. Indigenous North Americans harvested them for utilitarian purposes. They are high in protein and minerals and have many medical applications, since they have analgesic, antirheumatic and disinfectant properties. Today, the seeds of the sunflower are used worldwide for food, soaps, paints, and cosmetics, among other things.

OUR INHERITED WISDOM

From about the sixteenth century onward, sunflowers have weathered being in and out of favor among poets, gardeners, painters, writers, and literary and religious movements. They have been praised for their radiant beauty, their broad amber discs surrounded by a fringe of glistening yellow petals. Folklore depicts the sunflower as "false riches," "pride," and "haughtiness," as well as "vitality," "joy," and "extreme devotion."

With the Latin name *helianthus,* which comes from the Greek words *helios* meaning "sun," and *anthos* meaning "flower," the sunflower is touted as having heliotropic properties, as it follows the light of the sun from east to west. This has birthed some of the most lasting and deepest symbolism of the sunflower: an eternal hope that humanity will shift our focus away from devastation and toward lasting love and truth.

The sunflower is a brilliant reminder of some of the most vexing questions about who we are as humans, why we exist, and what is our relationship with the greater universe and the everlasting supreme. Like an individual sunflower seed, we can only know our closed reality. Yet, if we break open from our shell, we are able to see that we are part of an intricate spiral of thousands of seeds held together within, and by, a sunny, exuberant orb.

SUNFLOWER

PRACTICE

This practice supports awareness of your inner light.

Prepare—
- Standing.
  - Stretch your arms and hands overhead.
    - Feel as though you are reaching down through the soles of your feet and then upward through your fingertips.
  - Staying rooted, yet evenly lifting yourself up, relax your arms by your sides.

Practice—
- Still standing.
  - Bring your palms together in front of your heart.
    - Bow your head slightly and lower your gaze to your fingertips.
    - Silently acknowledge your deepest self. If you have a religious belief, bow to that.
  - With an inhalation, reach your hands down alongside your body, then arc them outward and upward like rays of the sun.
    - Imagine as though, as you reach out from your heart, you are a beautiful expression of your deepest truth in all your actions, thoughts, and words.
  - With an exhalation, join your palms above your head and then lower them to your heart center.
- Repeat this several times.

OUR INHERITED WISDOM

Transition Back into Your Day—
- Sit quietly for several minutes.
  - Watch the gentle movement associated with your breath.
    - Imagine the inner light is radiating outward from the center of your heart with each inhale.
    - And, on each exhale, your breath moves back inward, stoking the glow of your inner light.
  - Pause.
  - Remind yourself that you are a seed within a spiral of seeds and, like the sunflower seed, your personal shell may obscure your view of the whole. No judgment, just a gentle reminder.
- When you are ready, return to your day.

SUNFLOWER

TREE

There's a tree that existed before the woods,
in age twice as old.
Its roots suffered as the valley changed,
its leaves deformed by wind and frost.
People all laugh at its withered aspect,
caring nothing about the core's beauty.
When the bark is all stripped off,
only essence remains.

Hanshan
Trans. by Tony Barnstone

This morning I was introduced to Lillie. While the name might sound like a new app or clothing line, Lillie is something more rare—she is a lithe, 101-year old woman. A tiny fraction of one percent of the world population is centenarian. The wrinkled face and hands give a hint of a century of living, but like most her age, she doesn't dwell on the hardships of epidemics and wars, or unrealized aspirations.

In tree years, Lillie would be a sapling among some species. In fact, the oldest recorded life of a tree is a spruce in Sweden aged about 9,550 years. Yet, Lillie's demeanor and attitude reflect the generosity of trees. She loves caring for her daughter and son-in-law, not because they house her, but

OUR INHERITED WISDOM

because she has a tree-like nature. There is a continual offering of strength, stillness, protection, nourishment, stability, refuge, receptivity, giving, and serenity.

Trees have long served as symbols of lasting wisdom. Most world cultures have tales of sacred trees. For example, in the ficus family: the pipal or bodhi (*F. religiosa*) represents happiness, longevity, and prosperity; the banyan (*F. bengalensis*), eternal life; and the sycamore (*F. sycomorus*), infinite connectivity between life and death. There are references to trees of life, knowledge, and perfection. And, there are promises that whoever knows the tree will be the knower of all truth. Their verticality is a reminder of our own rootedness in the earth, upright trunk and crown reaching toward the heavens.

As I read this poem by Hanshan, a 9th century poet-hermit, I felt as though I was near an ancient elder. Hanshan reaches across time and gathers together universal stories of our shared roots and lasting, spiritual nature. His imagery of a valley is symbolic of life itself as fertile and transitory. And, of the tree itself, it conveys a timeless essence, full of beauty and free of all rivalry and to amass more than is needed. I feel as though if I look carefully, I can find this or a similarly seasoned tree nearby. When I do, I will sit near its roots and simply listen.

TREE

PRACTICE

This practice supports awareness of receiving and letting go.

Prepare—
- Hold your hands in front of you.
    - Rotate your wrists 3 times in each direction.
- Close and open the fingers 3 times.
- Then, gently hold one hand in the other and squeeze. Repeat with the other hand.
- Shake out your arms, wrists and hands.

Practice—
- Repeat the following 3 times:
- Breath One:
    - Inhale—Reach your arms and palms out in front of you. Spread the fingers.
        - Hold the Inhale—Reach your arms to the sides, shoulder-high. Fingers are still spread.
    - Exhale—Arms still to the sides. Vigorously make a fist with the hands.
        - Release holding the fist. Spread out through your palms and fingers.
- Breath Two:
    - Inhale—Arms still to the sides. Let the hands relax.
    - Exhale—Lower your arms to your sides. Palms and fingers relaxed.
- Normal breath (for 6-12 breaths) – Arms relaxed at your sides.
    - (If seated, rest your palms on your thighs, palms upward.)

OUR INHERITED WISDOM

Transition Back into Your Day—
- Sit quietly for several minutes.
    - Backs of your hands rest on your thighs, palms upward.
- Imagine yourself as a tree, and that your hands are the roots.
    - Breathe.
        - Inhaling, imagine nutrients and fresh energy flowing inward through the fingertips and palms into your body and mind.
        - Exhaling, imagine that everything no longer needed is being released through the palms and fingertips.
        - Continue this rhythm of receiving and letting go for several minutes.
- Then, allow your breath to return to normal before returning to your day.

Divine Presence in All
INSECTS, BIRDS, REPTILES, AND ANIMALS

ANT

God
Blooms
From the shoulder
Of the
Elephant
Who becomes
Courteous
To
The
Ant.

Hafiz
Trans. by Daniel Ladinsky

A twig snapped under my boot. It broke the morning silence, causing a lizard to scurry across the trail into the nearby bushes. The leaves rustled and then there was a single sharp chirp, from a bird giving a note of alarm. The sounds made me aware that I was passing through a community of rocks, plants, and moving beings.

Instead of hiking immediately onward, I decided to pause. The appearance of the twig had gotten my attention. It hadn't come from the shrubs along the trail and there were no other trees with similar branches in sight. Even though I was unlikely to solve the mystery of its source, I felt a kinship with

OUR INHERITED WISDOM

the twig. Perhaps it was because I felt we both were visitors who had met along this mountain slope.

For my rest, I looked around for a place to sit. A large boulder seemed to invite me, so I patted its surface as if to say "thank you" before I sat down. It was then I noticed a steady stream of ants migrating toward the trail's edge, out of the line of footfall of future hikers. It was clear that had I not stepped on the twig, I would have unwittingly squished several ants.

Sages and saints across the world have long reminded us that the journey exists within each step. My experience on the trail reminded me of the words of the poet Hafiz about the "elephant who becomes courteous to the ant." Like all sacred words, there are many ways to interpret them, and often our interpretation will vary as we move through life. I would like to believe, in the end, that they inspire us to slow down, listen, unplug regularly, and recognize that at the heart of life is courtesy, kindness, love, and compassion.

It takes a lot of focus and effort to achieve the wisdom of wise beings, but we have many friends in our earthly community who are always there reminding us who we truly are. For example, the sun can remind us of our eternal essence of light. The natural elements can remind us of finding balance and harmony in the midst of ever-changing life. Animals and other creatures—great and small—can remind us to tread lightly, while more inert beings may remind us of steadiness without stagnation.

ANT

PRACTICE

*This practice supports awareness of navigating
the world with joy and reverence.*

Prepare—
- Find a quiet place in your home. Remove any potential distractions, such as your phone and computer.
- Standing. Reach your arms upward and stretch briefly. Then, return your arms down to the sides of your body.

Practice—
- Standing, acknowledge different parts of your body. As you do this, appreciate that your body helps you navigate the world.
  - Feet. Reach down toward the floor with knees bent. Cup your hands and imagine you are scooping up all material items that bring you love and joy. Stand, and reach your arms outward and upward. Open your palms to the sky and pause there, palms facing up. Turn your face upward. Imagine the love and joy of your things raining back down on you.
  - Navel. Open your hands in front of your belly. Imagine you are scooping your treasured emotions. Offer them up to the sky. Pause, hands and face upward. Let the love and joy rain upon you.
  - Heart. Open your hands in front of your heart. Fill them with your deepest desires. Bring your hands overhead, pause, and let your truth rain back over you.
  - Throat. Hold your hands lightly over your throat, as you gather your most precious words.

OUR INHERITED WISDOM

With your hands reaching upward, let the sweetness shower over you.
- Head. Cup your hands around the top of your head. Collect your most beautiful thoughts and best ideas. Reach your hands upward, let go, and let the love, joy, and beauty pour over you.

Transition Back into Your Day—
- Seated. Sit quietly.
- Make a vow that at least once during the day you will remember that through your body you have many ways to be attentive and considerate to other beings that invisibly support your life.
  - For example, as you enter a room—even if you have entered that room a thousand times before—pause and appreciate some part of the room.
    - Appreciate the source of the materials, such as the wood in the floor that comes from trees, or the wool in the carpet that comes from sheep.
    - Appreciate all those who built the space and maintain it, even if that might be you.
- When you are ready, transition back into your day.

ANT

BUTTERFLIES

To wake at dawn with a winged heart
and give thanks for another day of loving;

To rest at the noon hour and meditate
love's ecstasy;

To return home at eventide with gratitude;
And then to sleep with a prayer for the
beloved in your heart and song of praise
upon your lips.

Khalil Gibran

In the midst of the current human and natural disasters, it seems almost naïve to be optimistic about our collective future. Yet, around the planet daily miracles and feats are performed not only by people, but also by some of the smallest life forms.

Butterflies, for example, have been around for an estimated 50 million years. These beautiful insects exhibit the capacity for change more than another living creature. They crawl as caterpillars, cocoon, and then, lightly float away with delicate and colorful wings. Species, such as the Monarch, can travel several thousand miles. They are pollinators for some plants, and indicators of healthy ecosystems, as well as controllers of aphids and other pests.

OUR INHERITED WISDOM

Across cultures, butterflies represent beauty, renewal, simplicity, keen vision, peace, playfulness, and the interdependence of all life. They represent individual transcendence, from the societal pull toward gossip and dissatisfaction to a mind immersed in humble gratitude, kindness, and joy.

This metamorphosis takes personal effort. There is an ancient story of a butterfly that died when a person, intending compassion, tried to free it from its pupa by cutting it open. But, unfortunately, this disrupted the natural cycle of the butterfly, which needed to build its own wings and free itself from the cocoon. Transformation happens from the inside out.

I feel butterflies remind us of our kinship with nature and other species. Like butterflies, we are at different stages in our life cycles. Some of us are enveloped in our cocoon, and some of us have freed ourselves of tendencies to cling and hang on. Others are sweet reminders that *each* moment is filled with the grace of unseen love.

BUTTERFLIES

PRACTICE

This practice brings awareness of the rhythmic nature of the breath.

Prepare—
- Set the intention to go offline for five to ten minutes. Clear your environment of digital and audio distractions, e.g., turn your digital gadgets to airplane mode, and remove your wristwatch.
- Find a comfortable seated position—either on the floor or in a chair—and gently settle into the earthly support beneath you. Your eyes can be closed, or open with a soft gaze.
    - Allow the backs of your hands to rest on your thighs.
- Wrap the fingers of your right hand around your right thumb.
    - While continuing to hold the right thumb, do the same with the left hand. (If you are left-handed, begin with the left hand and then add the right hand.)
    - Lovingly hold both thumbs and breath for a few breaths.

Practice—
- Move your thumb and individual fingers in sync with the breath:
    - Inhale—
        - Gently open your palms, thumbs, and fingers to relax into a soft and open hand.
            - Return to this hand position with *each* subsequent inhalation.

OUR INHERITED WISDOM

- ○ Exhale—
  - ■ Three exhales for each finger while lightly touching the tip of your thumb (simultaneously on both hands).
  - ■ With the tip of your *index* finger.
  - ■ With the tip of your *middle* finger;
  - ■ With the tip of your *ring* finger; and,
  - ■ With the tip of your *little* finger.
- Move your entire hand in sync with your breath:
  - ○ Smooth Inhale and Exhale—
    - ■ With minimal effort, allow your entire hand to gently open with each inhale and relax inward with each exhale.
      - • Imagine that your inhales flutter outward from the deepest core of your heart to every cell in your torso, limbs, digits and skull.
      - • Imagine that your exhales quietly settle back into your heart center.
      - • Continue for as long as is comfortable.

Transition Back into Your Day—
- Stretch through your palms. Open your eyes if they were closed.
- Pause. Reflect on the rhythmic nature of the wings of a butterfly, first there is a symbolic release, and then gentle flight.
- Stretch out through your arms.
- When you are ready, return to your day.

BUTTERFLIES

COYOTE

> I know nothing, I understand nothing,
> I am unaware of myself.
> I am in love, but with whom I do not know.
> My heart is at the same time
> both full and empty of love.
>
> 'Attār
> *Trans. by C.S. Nott*

I awoke in the middle of the night to a high-pitched, beautiful sound. At four years of age, this was the first time I had heard this sound. My older sister, Gail, with whom I shared a room, didn't seem disturbed by the sound, so it seemed safe to just let myself be fascinated and listen. Almost as soon as it began, the odd refrain faded back into the nighttime silence.

The next morning, I was eager to share my newest encounter. On the farm, there seemed to be a plethora of nature's surprises: a fuzzy caterpillar appearing out of nowhere; a mockingbird adding a new song; or, a baby calf wobbling around soon after his birth. Every new discovery was a delight.

One of my friends was coming to visit that morning, so I waited to tell her my story. Rather than our usual shared glee, however, she began to sob as I mimicked the sound. In the midst of her tears, she told me that she had just lost her new puppy. It made me so sad that I began to cry, too. Then she

OUR INHERITED WISDOM

said it was a coyote that had killed her puppy. In that moment, I adopted her view of the coyote as dangerous, putting aside the awe that I had just minutes earlier.

When a coyote recently strode across the road in front of me, I remembered this story. It isn't every day that you see one, but it is becoming more common as coyotes move into cities and neighborhoods. As I watched the coyote pass through the traffic, I couldn't help but feel the awe that I had felt as a four-year-old. Perhaps I didn't feel fear or danger because I was observing the coyote from a car, but still, I could appreciate the way the animal's entire body moved in unison. It knew its own destination and seemed like a guest from the wild. In some First Nation cultures, the coyote is know as the Trickster, prompting us see things more clearly. Otherwise, we fall folly to not trusting our own experiences and instead, rely on others.

As the poet 'Attar reveals, our awareness of the "I" that we truly are arises out of our own experiences. Most of us have created a sense of who we are and what we hold dear based upon a collection of what we have heard or learned from others. In our desire to fit in and not cause ripples, we often stay within the bounds of our conditioned self. However, to reach the state of clarity of 'Attar and the great poets, prophets and sages, we are given daily nudges—such as by the coyote—to slow down, see anew, and surrender to the grace of life.

COYOTE

PRACTICE

This practice invites a sense of being showered by love.

Prepare—
- This is a seated practice.
    - Relax, as much as you can, the muscles around your face, neck and shoulders.
    - If seated on a chair, place both feet flat on the floor.
- Rub your palms together vigorously until you begin to feel warmth in your hands.
    - Curl your fingers and then stretch them a few times.

Practice—
- Rest your palms on your thighs.
    - Stay here for a few moments.
- Hands in prayer position at the heart:
    - Bring the palms together in prayer position at the level of your heart.
        - Pause for one or more breaths.
- Hands in prayer position overhead:
    - Palms still together, bring the hands above the head, fingertips reaching upward. Softly bend your elbows.
        - Pause with hands together overhead for one breath.
- Hands apart overhead:
    - Separate your hands and reach your arms into a "V" position overhead. With your elbows still soft, extend your palms and fingers. Imagine divine love flowing into your fingers and hands.

OUR INHERITED WISDOM

- Pause for one or more breaths.
- Hands still apart, moving hands from overhead to downward:
  - Hands overhead, move your fingers and hands as if they are dancing in the air.
  - Imagine that as your fingers move, you are being showered with millions of drops of divine love.
  - Slowly bring the hands back to your thighs.
- Repeat above sequence a total of three times.

Transition Back into Your Day—
- Sitting upright, let your hands rest comfortably in your lap.
- Pause for 6 or more breaths.
  - Your eyes may be closed, or open with a soft gaze.
- When you are ready, return to your day.

COYOTE

DOG

Not speaking of the way,
Not thinking of what comes after,
Not questioning name or fame,
Here, loving love,
You and I look at each other.

Yosano Akiko
Trans. by Kenneth Rexroth

It was a busy street corner. I stood at the curb, waiting for my husband Jay to pick me up. Cars sped by, each with the driver leaning forward, their gaze intense and hands gripping the steering wheel tightly. Pedestrians paused briefly near where I stood, looking to see if it was safe, and then quickly walking across the street while gazing down at their cell phone. No one seemed to notice flowering bushes, or the group of children wearing bright red ladybug jackets and bouncing along the sidewalk, accompanied by their caretakers.

    A large German Shepherd bounded up to the curb and sat down. A girl and boy arrived and hooked a leash onto the dog's collar. As the three of them crossed the street, my mind wandered to a favorite childhood book I had recently rediscovered. Actually, my youngest sister Jennifer had found it among a stash of books at the back of a closet in our parents' home. The book was amazingly well-preserved, with no musty smell or dust. The main characters were a German Shepherd named Rinty, a girl and her brother.

OUR INHERITED WISDOM

I encouraged my thoughts to come back to the flow of activity around me. But something inside me had shifted. The memory of that book gave me a sense of love so great, everything around me seemed to sparkle. The parade of drivers and pedestrians, the children and the plants and all the rest of life on that corner became a narrative of love. Just then, the German Shepherd turned to look at me.

My heart felt like it was exploding. His look was exactly the same as the dog Rinty, on the cover of the book that my sister had found: Rinty's bright eyes beautifully expressed all my heart had ever known as goodness. My mind tumbled again into the wonderful memory of the fictional dog that had overcome tough odds. The runt of a pedigree litter, he was considered to be too frail to be worthy of his ancestry. Fortunately, he was saved from being put to sleep by the brother and sister. Later, Rinty was kidnapped and sold to new owners, who lived thousands of miles away. Rinty again overcame the odds, escaped, and returned home by using his innate intelligence, courage, focus, strength, and love.

As I read words by poets such as Akiko, I am reminded that love's story is hidden within the fabric of life. It can't be found exclusively in any one word, book, person, or object; but still, each of those might hold the keys to love. I'm glad that my sister found the Rinty book. It gave me a way to see the completeness of life and, once again, brought me back home to the heart that always helps me navigate life. Over the next few weeks, I will remember Rinty, who was considered unworthy by worldly standards. However, he embodied ageless lessons that are beyond measure in the way he stayed true to the love in his heart.

DOG

PRACTICE

This practice supports awareness of ever-present love.

Prepare—
- Find a comfortable seated position away from possible interruption from your electronic devices.
  - Notice the surface beneath you. Touch that surface with your fingertips, acknowledging the earth that is always supporting you.
- Notice the space around you. Reach your hands outward and upward as though touching the space with your fingertips. Acknowledge the air and the space that is always supporting you.
  - Notice your limbs, torso, and head. From your feet up to your head, lovingly pat your body. Acknowledge your body, which is always there for you.
  - Notice your face. With both hands, lovingly touch your nose, mouth, cheeks, eyes and ears. Acknowledge the sensory organs for smell, taste, touch, sight, and sound; they are your doorways to the world.

Practice—
- Place one palm over your heart and the other hand on top.
  - Relax through your shoulders, face, arms, and hands.
  - Close your eyes, or, if you prefer, leave them open in a soft gaze.
  - Acknowledge that your innate (heart) wisdom is always guiding you and supporting you.

OUR INHERITED WISDOM

- Leaving your hands over your heart:
  - Imagine as though beneath your hands, there is an abundant stash of love in your heart. For twelve breaths:
    - Inhaling.
      - Imagine the love radiating out from the core of your heart to the inner surface of your body.
      - Silently say the word "love," letting the length of the l-o-v-e stretch to meet the length of the inhale.
    - Exhaling.
      - Imagine the love seamlessly flowing back into the core of your heart from every cell in your body.
      - Silently, say the word "love," letting the length of the l-o-v-e stretch to meet the length of the exhale.
  - If you have time, continue for another twelve breaths, as follows:
    - *Inhaling.*
      - Imagine the love seeping into your body through every pore and all your senses (eyes, nose, ears, skin, mouth).
      - Silently say the word "love," letting the length of the l-o-v-e stretch to meet the length of the inhale.
    - *Exhaling.*
      - Imagine the love seamlessly flowing out through your pores and senses.
      - Silently say the word "love," letting the length of the l-o-v-e stretch to meet the length of the exhale.

Transition Back into Your Day—
- Sit quietly for a few moments.
- When you feel ready, return to your day.

DOG

GEESE

Whatever happens. Whatever
what is is what
I want. Only that. But that.

Galway Kinnell

It seemed odd that a gaggle of wild Canadian geese was lolling around and grazing by a nearby pond in the late afternoon. Usually they fly in early in the mornings and leave by mid-afternoon. But today, they were peacefully moseying around, appearing content to be where they were.

"It's a full moon," explained a friend who is a bird-watcher, when I shared my concern that the geese hadn't left for the day. On a clear full moon day, geese often continue to feed under the moonlight. As the lunar cycle wanes, they return to their normal arrival and departure times.

Wild geese are best known for their v-shaped flight pattern, which allows them to effortlessly migrate thousands of miles to nesting and breeding ground. They move with loving synchronicity. The wing flap creates an uplift for the bird immediately following. When one goose is injured, another stays with it. The ones in front regularly change positions with the ones in back, encouragingly honking to the ones ahead.

Even with their amazing flying capacity, I was struck by the quiet presence of the geese along the shoreline. The sense of caring support that carries them across the sky was

OUR INHERITED WISDOM

noticeable even on the ground. They moved together across the lawn, several geese forming one graceful unified movement. It is no wonder that they ascend to great heights.

The ability of the geese to seemingly be at peace reminded me of this poem entitled "Prayer" by Galway Kinnell. Perhaps it was because they were silent on the ground, attending to their needs and nothing more. Most of nature is this way—following ancient patterns—where they only want to be *that*, just *that*. As humans, we are intrinsically woven into this natural fabric, yet we forget that we share the air, soil, sunlight, and waters with one another as well as with multiple other species.

My father, who lived into his nineties, wisely began his days with a prayer to know the difference between his wants and his needs, and to take only what is needed, not more. This is not an easy path to follow, but it allowed him to have ample room for laughter and for interest in the stories of strangers. Like most in earlier generations, he had missed the escalation of longings and wants that has been cultivated by the growing marketplace. Thus, his wants for material possessions were mostly work-related, leaving him freer than most to simply long for peace.

May we all be like the geese and ascend to the loftiest heights. As humans, we have the gift of this life to learn to know what we truly want, and to live our lives accordingly. Personally, I want to inhabit that open space between the words. I want to be in that sky-space that holds and sustains all of life. *That*, and only *that*.

GEESE

PRACTICE

This practice invites you to cultivate inner peace.

Prepare—
- Please find a comfortable seated position.
    - If you are in a chair, rest the soles of both feet on the floor.
- Invite awareness of your breath.
    - Ask yourself, "How is my breath today?"
        - There is no right or wrong; just observe how your breath feels today.
        - If comfortable, softly close your eyes. Otherwise, leave your eyes open in a soft gaze. Breathe.
- Allow the palms of your hands to relax, upward, on your thighs.

Practice—
   Part I
- Just breathe.
    - With each inhale, silently say, "May I be peaceful. May I be joyful. May I be free."
    - With each exhale, silently say, "May I be peaceful. May I be joyful. May I be free."
    - Continue for eight to twelve breaths. Pause when needed.
- Sit quietly for several minutes.

OUR INHERITED WISDOM

Part II
- Receive and release peace, joy, and freedom.
  - Bring your left palm over your heart center. Rest the right palm over the left.
    - Silently say, "Thank you. I am peaceful. I am joyful. I am free."
    - Let go of the words.
      - Imagine you are filled with peace, joy, and freedom. Every cell of your body is filled with peace, joy, and freedom.
  - Gently, reach your palms out to the sides of your body (palms upward).
    - Imagine are a fountain of peace, joy, and freedom flowing from your heart out through your fingers into the world.
      - The fountain is eternal. You are an eternal recipient and source of peace, joy, and freedom.

Transition Back into Your Day—
  - Bring your palms together in front of your heart, in prayer position.
    - Pause in silence for a few moments.
  - Take your time returning to your day.

GEESE

HUMMINGBIRD

True love gives us beauty, freshness,
solidity, freedom, and peace.

True love includes a feeling of
deep joy that we are alive.

Thich Nhat Hanh

As I turned the corner toward my front door, a streak of color darted before my eyes. A soft hum penetrated the air, giving me the sense that I had entered an ancient temple infused with the peaceful chanting of *Om*. Almost instantaneously, I felt a childlike joy in this encounter with a hummingbird.

It is not surprising that this tiny bird sparked such feelings of delight. Hummingbirds playfully move through the air as if they are dancing with the light. Their aerobatic agility allows them to fly in all directions at full speed. With their fast wingbeat—50-80 beats per second—they can appear to stand still when they hover, as though suspended in time. This mirage of timelessness is echoed in their wings' figure-eight pattern, or the symbol of immeasurable and boundless infinity.

The sign of infinity represents eternity and balance. In more modern times, it brings timeless messages of true love and the gifts of strength, vitality, peace, and beauty. There is simultaneously a sense of the divine and the eternal grace of

OUR INHERITED WISDOM

existence. It is buoyant and unburdened by the heaviness of brooding over the past or the tension of worry over the future. It offers a reminder to lighten up and tune into the heart of life.

The hummingbird offers the tranquil messages of infinity, and fills us with gratitude for the sweet nectar of life. With acuity for authentic sweetness, the hummingbird eloquently slides its slender beak past the bitter exterior of plants to fully delve into the sweetness within. Its inward journey not only retrieves the nectar, but harmoniously gives back to the plant by pollinating the flower.

Sages, saints, and masters such as Thich Nhat Hanh are like hummingbirds, transmitting timeless wisdom and filling us with awe and hope. It is as though they lovingly nourish us with seeds of truth. The beauty of nature and their wise words are reliable doorways into our deepest and most sincere selves.

Hummingbird

PRACTICE

This practice supports the sweetness of loving abundance.

Prepare—
- Choose a place where there is minimal ambient noise or light. Put your digital devices out of reach and turn their volume off.
- Sit in a comfortable position, either on a chair, or the floor. Note: This practice could also be done resting on your back. Make any adjustments you need for comfort.
  - If you sit on a chair, rest the soles of your feet evenly on the floor.

Practice—
- Slowly shift your attention to your breath. Notice the gentle expansion in your torso on the inhalation, and the release on the exhalation.
  - Gradually lengthen your breath, keeping it smooth and even.
  - The following has *three segments*, with *three breaths in each segment.*
  - Breathe throughout—the guidance for the three breaths with each segment is:
    - Inhale—Say to yourself, "Every part is loving abundance."
    - Exhale—Let the feeling of loving abundance settle into every cell.
  - The three segments with the above breath pattern:
    - Sweep your awareness from:

OUR INHERITED WISDOM

- - - your hips to your legs to your feet, and to the tips of your toes;
    - your shoulders, torso, arms, and toes;
    - the top of your head, body, arms, and toes.
  - Gently breathing, let loving abundance seep inward:
    - For example, let love seep into your tissues, muscles, organs, neural and circulatory networks, respiratory system, and bones.
      - If you find areas that feel heavy or agitated, just notice them. Imagine that you can gently reassure them that you have noticed them, yet, for now, they may simply rest in loving abundance.
    - When you feel ready, invite your awareness to shift to the center of your chest, symbolically, the deep and timeless core of your being.
      - Imagine that deep within you is a beautiful, vast space that stretches into infinity. It is filled with loving abundance.
      - Let your awareness delve into that sweetness, enfolding and enlivening you with the nectar of loving abundance.
      - Remain here for a few breaths.
  - Bring your palms over your heart, one hand on top of the other. Imagine as though this gesture is sealing in the vitality, peace, and joy of loving abundance.

Transition Back into Your Day—
- Sit quietly for a few minutes.
- Perhaps set an intention to notice "loving abundance" as you move throughout your day.

Hummingbird

- For example, be aware of loving abundance in the water flowing from a faucet; the food that you prepare and eat; your friends and family; your home and belongings; the air you breathe; and, all of nature.
- You live in the midst of living abundance. You are loving abundance.
- When you are ready, return to your day.

SQUIRREL

If you want money more than anything,
you'll be bought and sold.

If you have a greed for food,
you'll be a loaf of bread.

This is a subtle truth:
whatever you love, you are.

Rumi
Trans. by Coleman Barks

Wildlife often grazes on a hillside outside our kitchen window. Yesterday, as I was eating breakfast, a squirrel romped across the hill and then scurried up a tree. After a few minutes, the squirrel darted back to the ground and began digging up and moving some of its stashes. I am sure that whatever they are, there will be just enough food to sustain its nourishment through the winter.

I marvel at the wild species' ability to use only what they need. Unlike humans, they rarely over-consume. Most animals are careful with their food sources, i.e., not over-grazing, polluting, exploiting, or destroying, but leaving enough to foster regeneration. Like the squirrel, they accurately predict

OUR INHERITED WISDOM

what will carry them through leaner times. Overall, they model timeless principles of non-greed, trust, respect, patience, responsibility, and authenticity.

Abundance is something that is innately understood and often shared in the natural world. As humans, we struggle to reconnect with this fundamental aspect of our existence. It isn't surprising that, universally, various religions warn us to beware of the pursuits of gluttony, pride, lust, envy, anger, greed, and sloth. Most of us likely feel as though we have these negative traits in check, especially since we can readily identify them in others.

However, with almost every aspect of our life orchestrated by commercialism—from pregnancy to sickness to death—the words from the poet Rumi are even more valid now than they were during his lifetime in the 1200s. Slothfulness, for example, has seeped into our lives in the guise of convenience. Gluttony seems to be woven into the comforts of our paved, plastic, metallic world.

Rumi's words "whatever you love, you are" inspire hope that we as humans can once again fall in love with what has been there all along: not only the eternal love of the divine, but that love expressed in every aspect of nature. I endeavor to reclaim that gift of our humanness of being joyfully alive, and in kinship with our sacred world. To do that, I choose to intentionally cultivate and "squirrel away" those subtle qualities that engender peace and love, e.g., kindness, gentleness, and respect.

SQUIRREL

PRACTICE

This practice supports gathering eternal, loving values.

Prepare—
- Find a comfortable seated position.
  - If you are seated on a chair, place the soles of both feet on the floor.
- Quietly notice your surroundings—that which is beneath you, around you, and above you.
- Notice your body, sense of self, and breath.
- Say "thank you" to all.

Practice—
- Choose one inner value that you would like to befriend.
  - For example, gentleness, calmness, kindness, or lovingness.
    - Take your time.
      - Just like a squirrel that patiently collects and stores acorns, you are embracing one inner value to guide and support you in life.
- Breathe sweetly, as though sipping in the air.
  - Inhale: Imagine you are greeting your value and inviting it into every aspect of your being.
  - Exhale: Imagine as though your value is comfortably settling into every dimension of who you are.
    - Allow yourself to trust that, like a well-cared-for plant, your value will steadily grow and deepen its roots.

OUR INHERITED WISDOM

- Let yourself be absorbed in the sweetness of your value for as long as is comfortable.

Transition Back into Your Day—
- Place your hands over your heart to seal in your friendship with your eternal value.
- When you are ready, return to your day.

SQUIRREL

TURTLE

The great sea has set me in motion,
set me adrift,
moving me like a weed in a river.

The sky and strong wind
have moved the spirit inside me
till I am carried away
trembling with joy.

Uvavnuk

A small object bobbing on the surface of the waves had captured my attention. Instead of moving rhythmically in and away from the shore, it would sporadically disappear. Intrigued, I decided to end my walk along the bluff and watch it. And just in that moment, the object reappeared. It was a sea turtle.

Smiling, I was glad that I had noticed this ancient messenger signaling me to slow down and tune into the deeper currents of existence. This ocean-going turtle, called a leatherback, actually travels the currents across long distances. It is one of many hundreds of species of turtles with an innate affinity to be at home in the wild.

Not surprisingly, most world cultures embrace the turtle as a symbol of wise, caring persistence. Turtles are some of the

OUR INHERITED WISDOM

oldest living species, whose fossils date back 200 million years. Land turtles are known for their graceful patience, and their steady, consistent, and focused pace. They embody easeful timelessness, where everything gets accomplished, with minimal disturbance along the way.

Perhaps its most celebrated symbol represents both the path to, and the realization of, truth. For turtles with shells, their top is the earth's topography. Their body represents the fluidity of the waters of the earth. And, their base offers a horizon on which the sun and moon appear and disappear. Some turtles are said to be a map of heaven and the stars. The seven ridges on the leatherback turtle are likened to the strings on a lute that carry all the music of the world.

Turtles model the pathway to lasting truth as gradual and barely visible. Rather than rushing at or chasing after distractions, the turtle moves with calm persistence, one step at a time. Best of all, wherever they are, they are always home.

These poetic words by Uvavnuk echo the messages within the turtle's freedom. Pursuing commercial desires and unhealthy cravings creates a hungry mind. With an agitated or unsettled mind, we can easily lose our ability to read the natural signposts that would lead us back to tranquility and away from harm to other species such as the turtle. When we slow down and sincerely persist, we regain the understanding that we have been swimming in the treasure we seek all along.

TURTLE

PRACTICE

This practice invites an awareness of our four limbs.

Prepare—
- Remove your shoes. Place your electronic devices out of sight and hearing.
- Sit quietly on a cushion on the floor, or in a chair.
  - If you are in a chair, allow your feet to rest on the floor.
  - With your eyes gently closed, or open with a soft gaze, let yourself savor this moment of calmness.
- Invite your breath to be effortlessly smooth and easy.

Practice—
- Notice your hands and your feet. Appreciate their shape, their structure, and how they help you navigate through life.
- Slowly explore the movement of your wrists, fingers, and hands.
  - For example, you might rotate your wrists around or wiggle your fingers.
- Slowly explore the movement of your ankles, toes, and feet.
  - For example, your might rotate your ankles around, stretch the toes apart and squeeze them together.
- Standing, explore moving all four limbs freely.
  - For example, you might lightly shake out one limb at a time, or imagine that you were swimming through air.
- Notice the space and surface beneath you.

OUR INHERITED WISDOM

- Then, walk gently along that surface and through the surrounding space.
- Imagine you are able to talk to and listen to your environment through your limbs.

Transition Back into Your Day—
- Sit quietly. Relax your face, hands, and feet.
- When you are ready, return to your day.

TURTLE

Divine Presence in All
OCEANS, RAIN, RIVERS, AND TEARS

BLUE PLANET

Are you jealous of the ocean's generosity?
Why would you refuse to give
this joy to anyone?

Fish don't hold the sacred liquid in cups.
They swim in the huge fluid freedom.

Rumi
Trans. by Coleman Barks

The plane began its journey over the Pacific Ocean. My husband Jay and I were traveling from California to Hawaii for a business trip and I had a window seat. As we rose in the sky, the coastline disappeared and the waves were no longer distinguishable. Just before we entered into the clouds, the view was an unbroken expanse of blue. It reminded me of the iconic photo "Blue Marble" showing earth as a blue dot in the midst of the universe.

There was something magical about the vast blueness. From the plane, the sky and ocean appeared as a continuous expanse of blue. It was as though our plane and all earthly existence were held in an eternal embrace. From this aerial perspective, an exquisite blue seemed to seamlessly envelop and sustain all of life.

For a number of reasons, the rivers, oceans, and sky

OUR INHERITED WISDOM

appear blue. The blue waters and air constantly hug us, inside and out. We depend on them to live. Like our planet, our bodies are approximately 70 percent water. And, from the moment we are born until we die, we breathe. Throughout life, there is a rhythmic movement of fluids and winds across the surface of the earth and within our bodies.

I feel that the pervasiveness of the color blue reminds me of the grace of life. It is no wonder that among its symbolic meanings, blue represents wisdom, trust, and heavenliness. When I rest on my back and look up at a clear sky, or gaze out on the ocean, the wide stretch of blue stimulates feelings of wholeness, peacefulness, and tranquility. There is a sense of merging into the sacred home to all.

For me, the blueness of our planet is a reminder that humans are a part of the intricate web of planetary life. Simultaneously, it is a reminder of the ubiquitous presence of divine love. The blue represents the sky or ocean that generously holds life. It represents the limitless, eternal love that holds all other forms of love. The poet Rumi offers a sweet invitation to live free of clinging and grasping: instead, accept and surrender into the boundless generosity, both seen and unseen.

BLUE PLANET

PRACTICE

This practice supports awareness of your water-nature.

Prepare—
- Find a quiet spot, inside or outside. Place your devices on airplane mode.
  - Ideally, remove watches and any trackers from your wrists.
- Standing, for at least a minute, sway and move as though you were a seaweed in the ocean.
  - Don't worry about how you look. Let yourself feel the fluidity.
  - If outside, notice the blue in the sky, or the waters.

Practice—
- Imagine you are stepping into the calm, clear blue ocean.
  - Take your time, and slowly immerse yourself in the water.
  - Breathe smooth and easy. This is an imaginary ocean, so you can completely submerge yourself in the blue expanse.
- Feel the peacefulness on the surface of your body and head.
- Imagine that peace seeping into your pores.
  - Feel as if your entire being were taking one long drink of tranquility.
  - Let calmness soak into your muscles, organs, bones, and deepest core.

OUR INHERITED WISDOM

- Imagine all you inner toxins and negativity completely dissolving until only the sparkling blue ocean remains.
- Let yourself feel like seaweed being swayed by the water. You can do this with or without movement.
  - If with movement, allow yourself to be moved.
    - If you tend to be active mentally, you may notice that your mind wants to initiate the movement. If that happens, tell your mind to relax and reassure it that it is still special, and that everything will be okay. Here, it can take a break.

Transition Back into Your Day -
- Sit quietly for a few moments.
- When you are ready, return to your day.

BLUE PLANET

THE FLOW

>Mountains are steadfast but the mountain streams
>Go by, go by,
>And yesterdays are like the rushing streams,
>They fly, they fly,
>And the great heroes, famous for a day,
>They die, they die.
>
>Hwang Chin-i
>*Trans. by Peter H. Lee*

I recently returned from a short tour of India. It was my fifth visit, yet it still filled me with fresh insight and perspective. There is a palpable sense that life is a series of natural and spontaneous changes. Everything finds a way to keep moving forward, seemingly trusting, and surrendering to, the flow of life.

India reminds me of the timeless importance of water and rivers to our earthly existence. Rivers were the site of early civilizations, and continue to offer water for drinking and irrigation, waterways, recreation, energy, and food sources for modern society. Hydrologists tell us that what they call the streamflow of rivers fluctuates 24/7. Even though they account for only a fraction of a percent of our fresh water, rivers are an integral part of the overall water cycle, sustaining aquifers and refreshing the oceans.

OUR INHERITED WISDOM

Rivers, water and oceans symbolize the ongoing current of all things. Creation stories in ancient cultures view life as borne of water. The Maori, Haitians, Sumerians, Japanese, Lithuanians, Nuxalk, and other peoples have water deities in their mythologies. The ancient Greek goddess of love, Aphrodite, arose from the sea. In Mesopotamia, a vast expanse of water represented absolute Wisdom. Many religious traditions use water for ritual cleansing. The River Ganges in India embodies the water of life and flows to the Infinite.

At its heart, water is an element of emotion, intuition, compassion, healing, rituals, cleansing, and the power of the feminine. It signifies the realm of spiritual and mental creation, growth, and realization. The poet Hwang Chin-i reminds us that flux is constant. Whether we welcome it or not, change happens. Obstacles occur. Even if we deny, or try to tame or control, its dynamic energy, life will still be impartial to our particular wants and desires. Like the river, life follows the natural call to surrender to the journey to the ocean.

It takes a conscious effort to reframe our perspective that our lives are interconnected with the ever-changing web of life. To do so means to swim upstream of modern thought, which was shaped by philosophers and others that humans are dominant over, and separate from, nature. Each of us needs to find our way home and surrender into the timeless wisdom of the prophets and sages teaching us that humans are part of the flow of all life. Our every thought and every action have a ripple effect on the well-being and freedom of all.

THE FLOW

PRACTICE

*This practice offers a gentle reminder that
life flows through your hands.*

Prepare—
- Sit quietly on a cushion on the floor, or in a chair.
  - If you are in a chair, allow your feet to rest on the floor.
- Release, as much as you can, any tension in the muscles around your face, neck, and shoulders. If you are seated in a chair, place both feet on the floor. Invite either a soft gaze or close your eyes. Allow ease and calmness to come into your hands and breath.

Practice—
Throughout the practice, try not to rush the breath or the movements. Repeat I—III, three times, depending on your energy and ability to focus. Begin with your index finger, then the middle, ring and little finger on each hand. Complete each part, i.e., I, then II, then III, on both hands—either one hand at a time, or together.
- I. Thumb to Fingertip
  - Exhale—Gently press the tip of your thumb to one fingertip, e.g., index finger.
  - Inhale—Extend that finger.
- II. Thumb to Fingernail
  - Exhale—Gently press your thumb to one fingernail.
  - Inhale—Extend the finger.
- III. Thumb to Whole Finger (thumb will be near second knuckle and the fingertip of that finger will

OUR INHERITED WISDOM

   simultaneously press into the palm).
   - Exhale—Press your whole finger with the thumb.
   - Inhale—Extend the finger.

Transition Back into Your Day—
- Open the eyes if they were closed. Maintain a soft gaze and allow the hands to rest comfortably on your thighs or in your lap.
- If you wish, take your fingertips, touch the bases of the palms lightly together in front of your heart.
  - Silently acknowledge your hands and their innate potential for healing and care for yourself and all life. Set a vow to be aware of how your use your hands, e.g., being thoughtful, discerning, and gentle.
- Pause.
- When you are ready, return to your day.

THE FLOW

RAINDROPS

Self inside self, You are nothing but me.
Self inside self, I am only You.

What are we together
will never die.

The why and how of this?
What does it matter?

Lalla
Trans. by Coleman Barks

It was a partly cloudy day. The weather prediction was mostly sun, so I decided to stroll at a nearby beach. When I arrived, I was delighted to see that the waves were calm; the receding tide had left a wide area of sand that was perfect for walking. As I meandered along the water's edge, a drop fell in front of my face. Instinctively, I looked up, partly expecting to see a gull overhead. A few more drops fell on my upturned face; sprinkles were coming from a passing cloud.

    The rain was so light that a group of children continued to play in the ocean. Their laughter inspired me to stop and watch their response to the passing shower. One girl began to imitate the raindrops landing on and then disappearing into the ocean. Repeatedly, she would plop full-belly onto the water, dive underneath, and then pop back up, giggling and holding her hands up to the sky. A couple other children were making their own rain by gathering ocean water in their palms, throwing it into the air, and laughing as the water fell back on them.

Raindrops signify all aspects of life—its cycles, emotions, interconnectedness, and even the gift of life itself. In some arid parts of the world, a single raindrop offers hope for replenishment and new growth. In areas that are prone to floods, rain prompts fear of destruction and loss. Different cultures associate raindrops with devotion, love, rebirth, compassion and calmness, as well as sorrow and difficulties. The drops also represent our human sense of separateness, and our longing to connect with other drops.

The children at the shore embraced the rain as a welcome playmate. Their play was a beautiful, natural expression of the multi-dimensional symbolism of rain. By being in the ocean, it seemed they were thoroughly immersed in the source of the all-pervasive, divine self.

As I read the poetic words by Lalla, I remember the delight of the children. Everything for the children at the beach seamlessly flowed together. There was no wondering how or why—it was all pure joy.

RAINDROPS

PRACTICE

This short practice invites awareness of childlike joy.

Prepare—
- Remove your shoes. Place your electronic devices out of sight and hearing.
- Sit quietly on a cushion on the floor, or in a chair. If you are in a chair, allow your feet to rest on the floor.
- Invite your breath to be effortlessly smooth and easy.

Practice—
- Standing or seated.
    - Give yourself a hug, holding your upper arms with the opposite hand.
        - Squeeze your arms and wiggle a little back and forth. Maybe even let yourself giggle.
    - Reach your arms and hands upward in a V-shape and look up.
        - Imagine that only the purest, sincere happiness is raining down on you. Let yourself be drenched in joy.
            - This can take one second, or as long as is comfortable for you.
    - Walk around as though you were splashing through puddles of joy. Smile.
        - Again, this can be a few moments, or as long as you like. It is only for you and your sweet, true self.

OUR INHERITED WISDOM

Transition Back into Your Day—
- Sit down quietly. Relax your face, hands, and feet.
- When you are ready, return to your day.

RAINDROPS

TEARS

What is it
you want to change?
Your hair, your face, your body?
Why?

For God is
in love with all those things
and He might weep
when they are
gone.

St. Catherine of Siena
Trans. by Daniel Ladinsky

Zoe had become a shadow of herself. The feisty, insightful artist that I had known was barely visible in the woman who sat across from me. It was almost as though she had taken her talent as an accomplished painter and transformed it into an image of who she thought she should be—inside and out. She had created a slender, coiffed mannequin able to talk about the weather, organizations she was supporting, and other general topics.

I felt sad. It was as though Zoe's uniqueness had been paved over. No amount of my weeping would ever bring back her drive for artistic work. Instead, like the flooded streets in a city after a storm, all the wild, unruly part of her that made her a great artist was now hidden beneath impervious layers. With her more intuitive and natural self sealed away, tears could no longer seep into her heart.

Being with Zoe reminded me of the gift of crying. When tears flow, our thoughts and voice are stilled. We cannot talk when we weep. There is only the rush of the waters from our eyes and the release within the recesses of our heart. Gradually, our own sorrows and attachments dissipate. We become deeply aware of the enormity of loss in the world—not just Zoe's voice and the works of art she will never create—but the multitude of disasters, tragedies, calamities, and injustices. Then, with pure knowingness and awareness in the heart, there is exuberant joy for the gift of tears and the clarity they bring.

Tears are a response of the heart. They represent moments beyond what the mind can comprehend. Around the world there are legends about the first appearance of tears and traditions that ritualize tears. Weeping has symbolized the overflowing of the waters of divine love. Tears are signs of ecstasy, grief, gratitude, elation, longing, and the grace of transcendence. When tears are cool to the touch, they are considered an expression of one's being in a state of superlative happiness.

The symbolism of tears and weeping appears in the writing of saints and mystics around the world. To weep with longing for God was to know God. Unlike Zoe, who sought societal acceptance through crafting a safe and predictable persona, female mystic saints, like St. Catherine of Siena, often

TEARS

challenged societal norms and were fiercely independent. Rather than become immune to worldly suffering, they embraced it and served the poor and destitute. Their similarity to Zoe is that they took extreme measures to transform their minds and bodies—but for the purpose of being apt vessels of divine messages. Those messages continue to nourish those who weep for the divine.

PRACTICE

This short practice rests the eyes, the container for tears.

Prepare—
- Sit at a table, or any other even surface. (You will be cradling your head in your hands, with your elbows resting on the table.)
- Yawn and stretch out through the jaw. Then, stretch through your fingers and arms.
- Breathe in a relaxed and easy manner. Let go of any need to change your breath.

Practice—
- Rub your hands quickly together until you feel some warmth in your palms.
- Place your elbows on the table. Bend your arms so the palms are facing you.

- Lower your head toward your palms.
    - Rest your eyes (eyelids closed) in the heels of your hands.
    - Curl your fingers lightly over the forehead and hairline.
    - Let the thumbs curl lightly toward the temples.
- Easy gentle breathing. Relax through the jaw and shoulders.
- Appreciate a sense of deep release. Stay as long as feels comfortable for you.

Transition Back into Your Day—
- Eyes closed or with a soft gaze, move your head away from your hands into a normal position.
- Smooth, easy breath.
- When you are ready, quietly return to your day.

TEARS

WATER

> God
> dissolved
> my mind-my separation.
> I cannot describe now my intimacy with Him.
> How dependent is your body's life on water
> and food and air?
>
> St. Teresa of Avila
> *Trans. by Daniel Ladinsky*

I tugged my raincoat over a couple layers of sweaters and pulled on my boots. What had started as a few sprinkles was now in the third day of colder temperatures and heavy rain. The local creek waters have risen and dozens of new rivulets have appeared on the hillsides. In some places, the heavy earth has slid downward. Everywhere, there is the sound of water rushing, clattering, and at times roaring.

  The intense wetness had not only altered patterns in the landscape, but also all the local human activity. My puffy attire is just one little example. Traffic has slowed; parents are out with their children, helping them wade through the puddles; inside the grocery stores and coffee shops, there are no signs of cell phones. Most striking is that people are talking to and helping one another. Complaints, and the customary dialog of one-upping one another with grumbling, seem to have

OUR INHERITED WISDOM

magically disappeared. Instead, most of the conversations are filled with expressions of gratitude for being safe, and stories of kindness from neighbors.

These dramatic shifts in human behaviors are perhaps not so surprising when we reflect on the grace of our existence and its connection to water. On a purely physical level, a large percentage of our body is water. It is essential to key bodily functions: regulating body temperature; metabolizing and transporting nutrients; distributing oxygen; cushioning the brain and spinal cord; removing toxins; and enabling us to express deep emotions through our tears. Plants and trees need water to nourish us and other living beings with food and air. Water clears away our waste and is fundamental to some of our most creative and artistic adventures, such as painting with watercolors.

Our planetary home is also largely water. On our "blue" planet, water is ever-present. Water reminds us of the flow of life. Its molecules exist in the forms of solid, liquid, and gas. We recognize these forms as ice, fluids, and vapor/steam, but on a broader level, they represent the eternal realms of earth, atmosphere, and heaven. Universally, the ancients regarded water as sacred. For example, the Greeks honored the multi-dimensionality of water with more than two dozen gods and goddesses, e.g., for the ocean, rivers, etc. Water is at the heart of holy ceremonies and rituals to symbolically purify, cleanse, and bring closeness to the divine.

I like to think that those millions of raindrops are caring reminders of the divine connectedness of all things and beings. As humans, we often live separately from this awareness in

WATER

our human-centric lives. When we are removed from this awareness, our behaviors slip into harshness, destructiveness, and complaints.

The rain carries an ancient message of the purity and wholeness of all. And, as if to add an exclamation point to this message, the sky cleared soon after I went outside. Dewdrops glistened in the light on the grass and leaves and a double rainbow appeared.

PRACTICE

*This practice supports awareness of water,
to wash away unwanted emotions and nourish your energies.*

Prepare—
- Find a comfortable seated position. If seated on a chair, place the soles of both feet on the floor.
- Release tension in your hands and fingers by gently wrapping your fingers over your thumbs, squeezing, and then slowly letting go. Try hugging your thumbs 3-7 times. Then, relax your hands.
- Take a moment to acknowledge the watery fluids in your body, e.g., the blood in your veins, the subtle moisture in your breath.
  - Deeply inhale and slowly exhale a few times.

OUR INHERITED WISDOM

Practice—
- Imagine that your schedule is free and that you are outside in a comfortable, beautiful natural spot. For example, this could be in a garden, at the beach, on a balcony, or any-place there is water or plants.
- Feel as though the sun is shining and that it begins to rain, so lightly that you do not feel the need to move.
  - The temperature of the rain is warm and refreshing. Imagine that as the rain touches your skin, it generously carries away stress and any unwanted underlying emotions. Gently breathe.
  - After a few minutes, the rain disappears and a rainbow appears in the sky. Feel the air around you and any sounds of nature, such as the wind or a bird's song.
- Deeply inhale and slowly exhale a few times.

Transition Back into Your Day—
- Sit quietly for a few moments.
  - Hold your palms in front of you and cup them together. Imagine fresh water being poured into your palms. Gently raise the water up to your face and lightly brush your fingertips across your face as though you are washing it. .
  - Invite a sense of renewed joyfulness and energy.
- When you are ready, return to the activities of your day.

WATER

Divine Awareness and Mind
INTERCONNECTEDNESS

GARDEN

O how big is my beloved,
More than all the ones I know.
O how lively does my heart beat,
When I only see him glow.
Love can never be forced;
Treat it fondly, it will grow!

Swahili Wisdom

It is stormy outside. Conversations in the coffee shops and stores have shifted to exchanges about the local weather rather than national news. People almost seem relieved that the turn in the weather has given them a chance to connect with one another over age-old topics, such as winds and moisture.

Dramatic weather offers a raw reminder that life is unpredictable. Change is the norm. Yet, we can easily forget this, especially if our lives are comfortable, with a roof over our heads, regular meals, friends and family nearby, and we have our other basic needs met. The whirls in the weather reflect those in the rest of our lives—the socio-economic landscape, relationships, and the inner turnings in our mind.

The enigma of being human is that we live in and are part of the ever-changing cycles of the universe; yet we expect and yearn for constancy. The earth, atmosphere, and sky nourish and hold us. Even though we have a dynamic co-existence with the air, sunlight, rainfall, soil, plants and other

OUR INHERITED WISDOM

living beings, our impulse is toward dominance, control, and separateness.

From the earliest times, prophets and elders considered our earthly reality as a garden. The metaphor of a garden evokes the multi-layered and multi-purpose richness of life. When we embrace life as a garden, we become aware that the outer storms reflect those problems and fears that, like weeds, cause disruptions. Instead of nourishing the weeds by dwelling on the disruptions, we fondly plant and cultivate seeds of peacefulness and clarity. By being responsible and caring gardeners, our hearts flourish in compassion, kindness, and love.

A European medieval root of the word "garden" is an enclosed space. In older languages, a garden is a hidden place that is something more than an ordinary garden, i.e., a place for prayer or contemplation. Anyone who loves gardens can confirm that there is something transformative about being in a garden. The qualities of the plants, rocks, pathways, and waters re-awaken our sense that we not only live in a garden, but a garden lives within the depths of our being. Both are representative of divine Love that transcends all boundaries. And, as this anonymous poet shares, when we treat love fondly, it will grow.

Within the constant stormy changes, I intend to take more time cultivating the inner garden. That means being an active gardener of my own mind. That includes the disciplines of quietude and contemplation, awareness of not consuming more than I need, and avoiding clutter of the mind with random commercial inputs.

GARDEN

PRACTICE

This practice helps bring awareness to your interconnection with the earth.

Prepare—
- Find a comfortable seat.
- Relax the backs of both hands onto your thighs.
- Close your eyes and relax your face, hips and feet.

Practice—
- Take 7-to-10 calm, slow, calming breaths.
  - As you do, imagine that you can grow roots into the earth beneath you. At the same time, lengthen your spine upward and balance your head lightly atop it.
  - Imagine the roots getting stronger as you release tension across your shoulders and chest.
- Take another 7-to-10 smooth breaths.
  - Inhaling, visualize the earth's nutrients and minerals in your bones.
  - Exhaling, release the muscles away from the bones, all the way from head to toe. Feel yourself supported by, and integral to, the earth.
    - Notice if you are holding yourself up away from the surface beneath you; and consciously let go.
  - Sit quietly for several minutes.
    - Allow any thoughts or feelings to be absorbed into the ground. Surrender yourself in the way a plant does. All that you need, you have.

OUR INHERITED WISDOM

Transition Back into Your Day—
- Sit for 2-3 minutes, gently drawing your attention back to your breath.
- Bring your palms together in front of your heart and bow your head.
  - After a few moments, release the backs of your hands onto your thighs.
- Slowly lift your head up and gently open your eyes.
- Stand up, knowing that you are fully supported by, and an integral part of, the earth.

GARDEN

JOYFUL CONNECTEDNESS

> Spring overall. But inside us
> there's another unity.
> Behind each eye here,
> one glowing weather.
> Every forest branch moves differently
> in the breeze, but as they sway
> they connect at the roots.
>
> Rumi
> *Trans. by Coleman Barks*

Liza looked up at me with wide blue eyes. She seemed to be deciding on whether to hide behind her mother's legs or continue watching this new stranger in her home. She chose the latter, likely comforted by her mother's laughter and effusive welcome to me.

She reached down and offered me one of her toys. The floor was covered with small wooden balls and cups in different colors and sizes. In her hand was a red cup. Liza's mother, Ellen, and I understood this timeless, welcoming gesture. It was a simple but clear invitation from Liza to sit and join her.

Springtime offers a similar gesture to humans and other species. Each year, spring invites everyone to put aside the immediacy of the never-ending list of wants, and things to do, and, instead, join in reveling in, and praising, the gift of

OUR INHERITED WISDOM

existence. Like Liza, there is a fragile innocence to spring, as the grey landscape and bare trees turn into swaths of rich green and brilliant yellows, reds, purples, and pinks. By offering such raw beauty, Nature conveys a sense of trust that all are her kin and would only wish her longevity and well-being.

As we sat and played, I noticed a large tree with pink flowers outside the window. The branches were gently swaying back and forth. Some of the blossoms twinkled in the afternoon light. A squirrel scampered along the branches of another tree outside the window. It seemed that in that moment, the entire world was sharing, exploring and playing.

Small children often bring adults back in touch with the joyful interconnectedness of the universe. Without the filters or restrictions of language, they are attuned to the subtle, universal language of nature. Children have a keen drive to commune with the richness of natural textures, sounds and shapes. Their innate awareness inspires them to touch the plants, notice a creeping caterpillar, plop down in the sand or grass, and giggle at the sight of a certain bird or animal.

Children point to what people of the world's indigenous cultures have known from the onset of time. At its root, all life is an expression of the divine—all in one and one in all. Ancient sayings and poems continually remind us to notice and celebrate the sacred vitality pulsing within each moment. The gift of remembering our connectedness is tucked into the blossoms of spring, the patterns of the moon, the wag of another dog's tail, and the clarity in the eyes of a small child.

JOYFUL CONNECTEDNESS

PRACTICE

This practice supports awareness of your innate connection with the earth.

Prepare—
- When you are comfortably seated, rub your palms together briskly.
- Once you feel some warmth, rest the heels of your palms over your eyes.
  - Your fingers can lightly curl over your forehead toward the top of your skull.
  - Invite in a sense of ease and peacefulness. After a few moments, allow your hands to relax in your lap.

Practice—
- Imagine you are sitting at the base of a large tree.
  - The weather is a comfortable temperature, and the air is still.
  - The earth is supporting and nourishing both your body and the tree.
  - Deep beneath you is the core of the planetary home to all species.
  - The trunk of your body and the trunks of the trees receive and process the essential vitality from the earth, atmosphere, and heaven.
  - Around and above you, space supports your capacity to flourish.

OUR INHERITED WISDOM

- Breathe.
  - Revel in your kinship with the tree by breathing together—in and out, out and in.
  - Celebrate the earth that gives you both minerals and unseen layers of support so you may be upright and be a conduit of vitality in the world.
  - Honor the vastness of the sky and the gift of the sun. Praise the Divine.

Transition Back into Your Day –
- Stretch out through your arms. Then, relax your hands into your lap.
- Sit quietly for a few moments before returning to your day.

JOYFUL CONNECTEDNESS

NATURAL WISDOM

I know a cure for sadness:
Let your hands touch something that
makes your eyes
smile.

I bet there are a hundred objects close by
that can do that.

Look at
beauty's gift to us–
her power is so great she enlivens
the earth, the sky, our
soul.

Mirabai
Trans. by Daniel Ladinsky

I am lucky to live in a community where children play in the local parks. The toddlers seem to be the most enthusiastic about being outdoors, where they can practice their roaming skills. A typical sight is a tiny human running, with a parent rushing to catch up. It is as though there were some invisible leash tethering the two, so together that they move in unison.

Often, the child will trip and look up in wide-eyed astonishment. Just before he or she begins to cry, something draws the child (and the parent) into further joyful exploration of and attunement to the world. Dirt, grass, flowers, trees, sky, and all the animated beings, especially dogs, are part of a day's communing and learning.

I feel that I learn a lot from observing little people. They direct my awareness to the fact that humans are one of millions of species—with some estimates as high as eight million—that are invisibly linked together in the fabric of life. They are a good reminder that our biological existence is interwoven with the elements, and all the richness and complexity they support.

More and more, researchers are exploring how our entire well-being (physical, emotional, mental, social, and spiritual) is tied to having an active relationship with our human and non-human friends on this planet. Studies, for example, have shown that being in—or viewing scenes of—a nature-less environment can elevate anxiety and fear, and increase symptoms of stress, such as an accelerated heart rate. In contrast, being connected to our innate community can increase levels of trust, generosity, focus, openness, caring, respect and overall well-being.

The ancient saint and poet Mirabai reminds us to feed our soul with the surprises of seasonal beauty and mystery. Nature and children inspire us to keep our child-like experience of the basics of life—the earthly sources of our breath, nourishment, and shelter. Our souls sing with exuberance when we let go of who we think we are and begin to truly appreciate our kinship with nature, the elements, and other species. This requires a subtle shift away from any conditioned perspective that humans are superior to and separate from nature. Instead, we live in sync with the natural cycles and rhythms, being cared for, and respectfully caring for all planetary life.

PRACTICE

This practice brings awareness of our interconnectedness with other humans and species.

Prepare—
- Choose a day when you have some extra time in the morning.
- On the night before, just as you are ready to go to sleep:
  - Simply remember a moment in your day when you were aware that you were interacting with one of the elements, e.g., air, or the life of another species.
  - (There are no further instructions here, but follow your own intuition, e.g., ask yourself, how did that interaction enrich or support your life.)
    - If nothing comes to mind, don't worry. Just know that throughout the day, your existence has been supported in all sorts of invisible ways.

OUR INHERITED WISDOM

Practice—
- When you awaken from your sleep;
    - Notice what you first notice. No judgment, just noticing.
    - Before you arise, bring your awareness to the bedding on your bed. For just a few moments, reflect on your bedding. For example:
        - How does it feel on your skin? Soft? Scratchy?
        - How do you feel, taking the time to notice an everyday item?
        - For more analytical inquiry, reflect on:
            - What type of fabric is it? Cotton? Synthetic? If cotton, where was the cotton grown? Who grew the cotton? How did the cotton become fabric?
            - Where was the fabric made? How did it get to the factory or place where the bedding was made? Who transported it? What was it transported in, and what elements made the transport possible, e.g., metal, oil?
            - Who made the bedding? What do they eat? Where do they live? What elements support their lives, e.g., water.
            - Was it made in a factory? What elements were in the building walls, e.g., wood?
    - You don't need to spend a lot of time on this, nor do you try to find answers to the reflections. This is simply a way to help reawaken our awareness of and respect for the anonymous, intricate, and delicate web of our existence.

NATURAL WISOM

Transition Back into Your Day—
- Arise. If you have time, sit quietly for a few moments.
- When you are ready, move into your day.

THE PARK

Tranquil our paths
When your hand rests on mine in joy.
Your voice gives life, like nectar.
To see you, is more than food or drink.

Egyptian Wisdom
Trans. by Ezra Pound and Noel Stock

As I sat on a park bench the other day, I appreciated the sound of laughter and conversation from the people around me. There was a family, with three young children playing tag, an elderly couple, and a group of young adults sitting in the grass talking. Eyes were beaming and everyone seemed to genuinely enjoy being together.

Ten years ago, I might not have even noticed the jovial atmosphere. Not because I've necessarily become more aware over the past decade, but because it would not have been noteworthy to hear and see people happily conversing and interacting. The woman of the elderly couple rested her hand in the palm of the man's hand. The parents of the young children smiled at the sound of their children's voices. Even the trees, grass, and flowers seemed more alive.

While savoring this rare moment, I began to fantasize that somehow this group of humans had rediscovered the ancient secret to happiness. It seemed that if they had had

OUR INHERITED WISDOM

musical instruments, they would have made music together. Or, with paintbrushes, they would have harmoniously created a painting together. I could only fantasize so far; like me, they have shelter, food, and access to a clean public park. Yet, it was still striking that given their age, gender, and racial diversity, none were using digital devices. All heads were raised, hands free, happily engaged.

Humans have long experimented with and been influenced by our tools—from flint arrowheads to earthenware to typewriters and robots. None have been as overpowering and as alluring as our most recent inventions. It is rapidly becoming more commonplace to see humans interacting with screens and electronic devices than with one another or nature. The average person is unaware that this shift is radically narrowing—rather than widening—our capacity for true happiness.

Social bonding, compassion, creativity, contentment, and the general ability to be able to feel and care evolve from interating with other humans and living beings. Studies of the brain show that it needs dynamic interaction. While our screen world seems to be multi-sensory, studies show we have the illusion of being more connected, but are actually less aware and more isolated emotionally. We need real physical social interaction, like these people in the park, for well-being and inner tranquility.

The anonymous Egyptian poet from about 1500 B.C.E. summarizes the gifts within everyday touching, listening, and seeing. When we gently hold the hand of a loved one, no words are needed. The love and support is understood. Their voice

THE PARK

can bring us ease and a mere glimpse of their face can make us smile from the inside out. The seemingly mundane shapes our ability to trust, accept and explore, and to rediscover true joy.

PRACTICE

This practice helps renew your awareness of the sense of sight, hearing and touch.

Prepare—
- Sit where your digital devices are out of reach, sound, and sight. Even if they are in airplane mode, create some distance between you and them.
  - If you are in a chair or on a bench, place the soles of your feet on the ground.
  - Close your eyes, or have a soft gaze.
- Give yourself a gentle hug. If you feel fearful about being out of touch digitally, squeeze your upper arms with your hands and quietly reassure yourself that as a human, you are much more than your possessions.

Practice—
- Place the palm of one hand over the center of your chest.
  - The fingertips will point toward the opposite arm and shoulder.

OUR INHERITED WISDOM

- Allow yourself to explore whether there are any sensations or emotions. There is no right or wrong here. Just explore. For example, does the skin on your chest—even beneath the clothing—feel different when your hand is lightly touching the chest, resting there, or has moved away? How about the skin on your fingers and palm? Does it register different sensations if you let your hand completely relax and rest on your chest, versus if you lightly touch it? Are there any feelings you experience, such as comfort?
- Keeping that hand resting on your chest, rest the other hand on top of the hand on your chest. Explore sensations and feelings that you may have in your hands.
  - Breathe here for a few moments. Notice any movement in the torso associated with inhalation and exhalation.
- Lightly place your palms over your ears. Relax through the shoulders and eyes. Breathe five to six breaths. Notice the sound of the breath, and any sensations associated with having your hands over your ears.
- Lightly place your palms over your eyes. Fingertips are pointed upward and lightly curling over the top of your skull. Breathe five to six breaths. Notice any sensations while the hands are over the eyes and when you bring the hands away from the eyes.

Transition Back into Your Day –
- Rest your palms lightly in your lap.
- Breathe calmly and peacefully for as long as is comfortable.
- When you are ready, return to your day.

THE PARK

SPIRALS

For everything there is a season,
and a time for every matter under heaven:
a time to be born, a time to die...

Ecclesiastes 3.1

It seems I've been traveling quite a bit in the past couple of months. Between the ups and downs of the planes, I felt the undulating cycles of life. Spring flowers were in different stages of emerging and fading, new family members were expected as others passed on, graduations and reunions, snow and sunshine, and so on.

The ancient cultures understood the constant rhythm of the universe, one cycle gliding into the next. They experienced life as three threads spiraling three-dimensionally at lightning speed, clockwise and counter-clockwise, in different directions around an unchanging core. Messages about this awareness were recorded with spiral carvings in caves, tombs, rocks and pottery around the world.

Even though our modern-day world is composed of straight-edged shapes in our architecture, furniture, streets, and screens, we exist within spirals. In nature, there are eddies, whirlpools, wind and smoke patterns, and lunar and solar cycles. Swirls and florets appear in elephant's tusks, the horns of wild sheep, pine cones, flowers such as the sunflower and

OUR INHERITED WISDOM

the calla lily, snails, snakes, shells, and galaxies. Besides a corkscrew-like umbilical cord and coiled inner ear, our bodies have whorls and waves throughout. The natural forces of our existence radiate together in proportional harmonics defined by mathematical truths about the radiating movement of energy. Like an eternal song, everything vibrates together as a universal octave, with eight steps and seven intervals. We see the number seven reflected in the days of the week, the colors of the spectrum, and religious symbolism.

When I read this verse and/or hear it sung by the Byrds in Pete Seeger's "Turn! Turn! Turn!," I feel quietly peaceful within the dynamic spiraling of opposites. Polarities seamlessly somersault, fold and unfold. Blossoms appear and fade away, the in-breath cycles into the out-breath, and I begin to sense harmonic vibrating nature at play. Seemingly linear, isolated events—spring, summer, war, peace, birth, and death—are instead praises to life arising and returning to the eternal source. This inspires me to sing along.

SPIRALS

PRACTICE

This practice supports awareness of sound and inner spaciousness.

Prepare—
- Approach this practice with a sense of playful exploration.
- Hug all your bones by tightly squeezing all your muscles from head to hand to toe.
  - Hold the hugging for three to four seconds.
- Release.
  - Be sure to let go through the palms of your hands and across your forehead. Smile and breathe freely.
- Repeat two more times.

Practice—
- Open your mouth to create an extended *aah* sound.
- Imagine the pathway of the *aah* sound:
  - begins at your navel,
  - travels upward through your torso,
  - across the back of your throat and palate, and
  - out of your mouth.
    - You may find it helpful to gently drawn in and up on the abdominal muscles to strengthen the sound.
- First, imagine that your *aah* is bounding up a ladder.
- Then, imagine that your *aah* is bounding up a spiral staircase.
  - Play with the spiral of traveling counter-clockwise and clockwise, and broader at the base or narrower at the base.

OUR INHERITED WISDOM

Transition Back into Your Day –
- Take a few minutes to sit quietly.
  - Relax your hands and let them rest comfortably in your lap or on your thighs.
  - Allow your eyes to be open with a soft gaze, or gently closed.
- Invite the feeling of spaciousness into all your cells from the heart-center outward, from the tips of your fingers and toes and the crown of your head back into the center of your heart. Clarity, openness everywhere.
- In your own time, transition back into your day.

SPIRALS

Divine Awareness and Mind
SENSES OF SIGHT, SOUND, AND TOUCH

BEAUTY

Know
the true nature of your
Beloved.

In
His
loving eyes
your every thought, word, and movement
is always, always

beautiful.

Hafiz
Trans. by Daniel Ladinsky

In spite of the craziness in the world, I treasure the experience of beauty. Usually, it is when I am out in nature and become enraptured with the sweet fragrance of a blossom or the quietness of a new moon night. But it also can be in those moments of folding the laundry or sweeping away the leaves after a windstorm.

Beauty seems ever-present in those everyday occurrences, such as the graceful appearance of the sun above the horizon. Even on a cloudy or foggy morning, the light announces the arrival of a new day. Whether I notice or not, there is this ceaseless flow of beauty holding all of life.

OUR INHERITED WISDOM

For years, I associated beauty with the classical model of symmetry and harmony in which aesthetically pleasing meant being proportional in shape, limbs and face. Because I come from a family with short, round statures, it seemed beauty was an abstract ideal far removed from my sphere of life. Beauty was something I saw and appreciated in museums or on magazine covers, or even in my own artistic creations of drawings and photographs.

Poets, such as Hafiz, have kindled a broader and older appreciation of beauty. Rather than being about form, it is about the formless. Beauty is recognized as the subtle, radiant essence flowing through all that we do and say. I feel Hafiz points us to the beauty that seamlessly unites the finite and infinite, bringing a sense of endless joy and delight.

True beauty can awaken our awareness of the expansive presence of the divine and the realization that our intrinsic nature is beauty. This inspires me to take intentional pauses throughout the day and to sit in awe of the supreme beauty that simultaneously embraces and transcends all.

BEAUTY

PRACTICE

This practice invites awareness of beauty.

Prepare—
- Sit with an upright pelvis and straight spine on a firm cushion, or in a chair.
  - Let your shoulders release down in a relaxed way.
  - Let your hands relax on the thighs, palms upward.
  - Allow the breath to be even, slow, flowing, and gentle.
- Slowly allow the thumb to slide back and forth across the tips of the other fingers.
- Then pause. Allow the fingers and thumb to relax.

Practice—
- Move your eyes at a quick pace several times:
  - From left to right.
  - Up and down.
  - From upper right to lower left.
  - From upper left to lower right.
  - Circles each direction.
- Pause, with the eyelids lightly closed.
- Eyes open or closed, imagine you could look toward the center of your skull. It is as though you are looking at the pituitary gland. This is a soft gaze.
  - Allow your breath to be slow, rhythmic, flowing, and fine.
  - Stay for a few minutes.

OUR INHERITED WISDOM

Transition Back into Your Day –
- Bring your palms and fingertips together in front of your heart. Allow your inner gaze to move downward, as though you are looking at the center of your heart. Your eyes can be closed or softly open.
    - Acknowledge the beauty that you are, and the beauty in all things.
    - Take a few deeper, longer breaths.
- Relax your hands into your lap. Pause.
- When you are ready, return to your day.

BEAUTY

ETERNAL TOUCH

>As with lovers:
>When it is right, you can't say
>Who is kissing whom.
>
>Gregory Orr

White petals fell onto my hair. As three petals touched the strands I felt as though I had been kissed by spring with her abundance of flowers and blossoms. I let the petals linger in my hair, and savored the earth's constant, yet usually invisible, caress.

It is easy to forget we live on the earth. More and more, our ideal is to be removed from our earthliness. We eat with utensils, use sports equipment when we play outside, and have machines to make us more efficient and productive. Our newest forms of community are in cyberspace, where we value quickness of the mind and fluency in emojis to express our feelings. Spring and dramatic moments in Nature, such as sunsets, a gentle breeze, or the rush of rivers and waterfalls, can draw us back into our awareness of the gifts of air, water, and our innate connectivity with the earth and all life forms.

We are made to sense and be sensed. Biblical and other ancient references remind us we are made of the dust of the

OUR INHERITED WISDOM

earth. As earthlings, we need physical, not just our cyber, connection, in order to develop feelings of compassion, cooperation, and sharing. Even the simplest interchange between one living form and another can create a chemical form of communication. Humans touching one another can release the neurochemical oxytocin, or the love hormone, and create feelings of caring and kindness. A hug puts gentle pressure on the sternum, and studies indicate that the pressure on the chest or solar plexus can support emotional and physical well-being.

In some societies, touch is already stigmatized. An informal study of a group in a public place such as a coffee shop showed that people in English-speaking cultures touched each other once or twice over the hour. People in cultures that speak one of the Romance languages touched more than 100 times during the hour.

Gregory Orr's words fall onto my heart and touch me as the petals falling onto my hair do. They melt away any sense of separateness from life. As the barriers of fear and longing drop away, peace and love settle into each breath. There is no need to cling to the grand "I" that asserts itself with wants and desires. Instead, there is just sweet being, with nothing in particular to gain or achieve. Only the timeless kiss of life remains.

ETERNAL TOUCH

PRACTICE

This practice supports awareness of communing with the world through touch.

Prepare—
- Find a comfortable seated position. If you are seated on a chair, place the soles of both feet on the floor.
- Stretch out your palms and fingers. Then, gently squeeze each finger with the fingers of the opposite hand.

Practice—
- Slowly, lightly and gently stroke the palm and fingers of each hand a few times.
  - Stroke with kindness and gentleness.
  - Imagine you are touching the most beautiful thing on earth.
- Allow your hands to rest in your lap or on your thighs, with fingers relaxed and palms upward. Sit quietly and breathe softly and gently.
  - Imagine your breath caressing you from the inside out.
  - Receive this inner kindness. Savor it.

Transition Back into Your Day—
- Look at your hands. Say "thank you" to them for their ability to help you communicate with all life forms, and for their ability to give and receive kindness and love.
  - Silently vow that as you go about your day, you will be aware of your hands each time they touch something or someone.

OUR INHERITED WISDOM

- For example, when you pick up your fork before you eat, wash your face, fill your car with gas, hold your phone, hug a friend, or feel the rain or sunshine on your face.
  ◦ Before you re-enter your day, lightly touch your fingertips to your heart center, symbolically sealing in your vow.

Note: Although this practice focuses solely on the hands, you could create a similar practice for your lips, feet, or your skin as a whole.

ETERNAL TOUCH

HANDS

> Our hands imbibe like roots,
> so I place them on what is beautiful in this world.
>
> And I fold them in prayer, and they
> draw from the heavens
> light.
>
> St. Francis of Assisi
> *Trans. by Daniel Ladinsky*

Often as I tie my shoes, I think of my grandfather, Robert Vogt. He was the one who took the time to teach me how to tie my own shoes. What is memorable is his patiently helping me shape two loops, wrapping one over the other, and then pulling them apart. I got it on the first try, not only because of his easy method but because of his gentle, grandfatherly touch.

    Actions of touching and movement with the hands can have long-lasting effects. It is no wonder, since the nerve path endings of the hands occupy a large area of the brain. When we touch and feel something, especially with the fingertips, there is cerebral activity. Mystics and sages say that the entire mind and body—including the organs, the respiratory and other systems, consciousness, and imbalances or illnesses—are connected to the fingers and full hand.

OUR INHERITED WISDOM

When I read these words by the 13th century Saint Francis of Assisi, I feel the power of my hands to shape my entire being. If I relax my palms, inner tension releases. An open hand invites feelings of acceptance and letting go. If I bring attention to my fingertips and what they are touching, the touch becomes lighter and my forehead softens.

As I feed the birds in the morning and handle fresh vegetables, there is a symbiotic sense of existence. In all ways that we use our two hands, I am reminded of the delicate balance within duality—male and female, earth and heaven, seen and unseen, giving and taking, and much more. The most subliminal is hands folded in prayer, when the mind is calm and peace enters.

St. Francis suggests that our hands are like roots, with the capacity to simultaneously absorb and nourish, anchor, and nurture overall well-being. Our hands are visible roots. Rather than stretching underground, they cleanse, feed, and dress us. They shape and reflect our attitudes, habits, mood, and our relationship with each other, the environment, and ourselves. We can protect, heal, care for, greet, welcome, give, receive, love, share, create, bless, and let go with our hands.

These words of St. Francis inspire me to touch and move with the gentleness of my grandfather, knowing that touch has a long-lasting effect.

HANDS

PRACTICE

This practice supports a letting go of tension in your hands.

Prepare—
- Find a comfortable seated or reclined position.
    - If reclined on the floor, rest on your back, drape your legs over a cushion, and allow your heels to rest lightly on the floor.
- Stretch your palms and fingers wide. Then, gently shake your hands.

Practice—
- With the backs of your hands resting your thighs, allow your palms to softly open toward the sky. (If you are reclined, rest your hands on the floor.)
    - Invite a smooth, calming, gentle inhale and exhale.
    - From the tip of each finger, release and let go of unneeded tension across the finger and palm to the wrist.
        - Beginning with the little fingers on both hands, let go of the tension in the fingers on both hands, i.e., ring fingers, middle fingers, index fingers, and lastly, thumbs.
    - Keep a sense of relaxation in the fingers and palms, and let your hands roll over so the fingers are turned downward.
        - Silently speak to your hands. For example,
            - "Completely relax. You are free to do nothing but let go."

OUR INHERITED WISDOM

- • "I appreciate all that you do to care for me. You help me wash, nourish myself, navigate, communicate, create, give hugs…and much more."
- • "For now, I make no demands on you. You are completely clear and free."
- ▪ Let the communication through your hands fade away.
- ▪ Breathe. Imagine as though, with each breath, your hands and fingers release just a bit more.

Transition Back into Your Day—
- • Sit or rest quietly.
- • When you are ready, transition back into your day.

HANDS

LISTENING

> How
> Do I
> Listen to others?
>
> As if everyone were my Master
> Speaking to me
> His
> Cherished
> Last
> Words.
>
> Hafiz
> *Trans. by Daniel Ladinsky*

The plane to San Francisco from Denver was crowded. Our departure had been delayed a couple of times, yet everyone seemed amazingly calm—even the mothers with small children. I thought I was calm too, until I noticed that my mind was formulating comments on a conversation happening in the row behind me.

Apparently, my plane mates were planning a meal for an event. One of them mentioned the importance of appetizers. I felt my thoughts race into action, recalling all the children near and far who begin and end their day hungry, and the estimated billions of tons of food waste worldwide. But, just as my inner

OUR INHERITED WISDOM

dialogue was about to become a wildfire of thought, I decided to listen to the conversation.

One woman asked the other how she was doing. "It's been tough. I never felt such a large hole in my life." She went on to say how glad she was that she could chair the annual gala for the regional food bank, since there was such an increase in homelessness. She commented that after her daughter died (I hadn't tuned in on what had happened, however), she had a new appreciation of being there not only for like-minded friends, but also for complete strangers. "The world is really so small," she said.

I continued to listen and observed how my mind was shifting. The two women discussed their reasons for wanting an appetizer hour, expressing dismay at how seldom people even listen to one another anymore. They hoped that the people enjoying appetizers would engage with one another rather than with their phones screens. Sharing appetizers is a way to highlight the fragile web of life and the need for all of us to change our habits, they mused. Local vegetable farmers and chefs who are repurposing food that otherwise would have gone to waste would be featured in the appetizer segment of the meal.

Slowly, I let myself return to my thoughts. My mind, which thought it knew everything, really knew nothing. Where it expected to find threads of privilege, boasting, and insensitivity in their conversation, it found instead sincerity and loving graciousness. I felt calm where, before there had been an impulse to rush to judgment. If the sky outside the plane window could speak, I am sure it would have laughed

LISTENING

heartily. Through quietly observing and listening, my mind had re-discovered a calm spaciousness.

Ancient sages and poets like Hafiz inspire us to listen wherever we are, realizing that all of life is within everyone and everything.

PRACTICE

This practice supports awareness of listening and communicating from the heart.

Prepare (night before) –
- An hour before bedtime, turn off your screens, e.g., your phone, computer, and television. Let your mind relax.
- Ideally, use an old fashioned alarm and leave your phone in another room.
- Set an intention to awaken on your own, fifteen minutes before the alarm goes off. Also, set the intention to not engage in technology until after a short morning practice.

Practice (early morning) –
- Awaken on your own 15 minutes before the alarm goes off, ideally before sunrise.
- Before arising, listen to the early morning sounds for a few moments.
- Then, after a quick bathroom visit, find a comfortable place to sit quietly for the practice below:
  - Move your palms over the center of your chest.

OUR INHERITED WISDOM

- Notice the feeling of your hands touching one another and the symbolic spiritual heart center.
- Imagine that your true intelligence resides here, instead of in the mind. Appreciate this innate connection to eternal love and truth.
  - Reach your palms outward to the sides, as though your arms were wings of the heart. Take a full breath.
  - Sweep your arms overhead, and bring your palms together over your head, reaching upward to the sky.
  - With awareness, let your hands (palms together) move downward to your heart center.
    - As your hands pass in front of your face, invite an intention that throughout your day you will see, eat, and speak with a connection to love and the highest truth in your heart.
  - Return your palms to your heart center. Pause for a breath.
    - Repeat above cycle four more times.
- Reach your palms upward and cup them over your ears.
  - Invite an intention that throughout your day you will listen, see, eat, and speak with a connection to love and the highest truth in your heart.
  - Pause for a breath.

Transition into Your Morning—
- If you have the time, sit quietly for five minutes or longer.
- When you are ready, begin your day.

LISTENING

TOUCH

> God has never really spoken,
> though a thought once crossed His mind.
> It is the echo of divine silence
>
> we hear the birds sing, and that
> is the source of all
> we see and touch.
>
> Tukaram
> *Trans. by Daniel Ladinsky*

I savor the ordinary—the kind of stuff that you can find anywhere around the globe. There are the big things, like the horizon, clouds and sky, sun and wind. And, the little things, like the clatter of dishes, and ruts in the roadway. In between are the hugs and gestures that remind me of life's fragile beauty and interdependence.

The sense of touch keeps me in touch with my humanness as an embodied soul. Wherever my touch goes, my mind goes. I might even go so far as to rephrase "I am what I think" to "I am what I touch." Because touch is a complex process involving sensors in the skin, neuro-pathways, emotions, and messages to different regions of the brain, it is constantly feeding my identity. For example if I touch my palms together in prayer, calmness and equanimity are more pervasive.

OUR INHERITED WISDOM

Touching other humans and nature is a dynamic, multi-dimensional communication. We know that babies need touch to learn to bond, trust, and care. Touching living forms opens the doorway to compassion, gratitude, and kindness. We create through touch. Yet, now much of what we touch is a manufactured or processed product. This includes plastics, electronics, synthetic fabrics, and packaged food.

I believe that our individual, collective and planetary well-being is, literally, in our hands. Nearly 2,000 years ago, the Platonists prevailed over Aristotle and declared touch the most inferior of the senses. They felt that touch was too reactive to outer influence and deemed sight as the superior sense. I feel it is no accident that we find ourselves today in a culture where we are more drawn to touch objects that feed separateness rather than connectedness. For example, we touch silverware, steering wheels, phone screens more often than we touch the living objects that our ancestors touched, e.g., plants, animals, and natural water sources. Unwittingly, we are in an optic-centric civilization where we are losing touch with the modes of touch that deeply heal and nurture our capacity for civility.

To touch connects us to our earthly nature, but also opens us to our divine self. The Buddha, for example, points one hand toward the earth to bear witness to the enlightened realization that all is interdependent. This is most apparent when we consider the subtle touch of air in our nostrils, and the trees' contribution to our breath. No matter how sophisticated we become mentally, humans are part of, not separate from, earth, air, and nature. Our more loving and spiritual self arises out of the ordinary, not away from it.

TOUCH

When I read the words of Tukaram, I feel the grace of being touched. His words seem to have been written for our contemporary times, as a gentle reminder to reconsider what and how we touch. He evokes appreciation for staying in touch with that which sustains the world—seen and unseen.

PRACTICE

This practice support awareness of the gift of your hands.

Prepare—
- Approach this practice with a sense of playful exploration.
- Take a moment to look at your hands.
- Open the palms and hold them comfortably in front of you, with the palms facing you.
    - Move your fingers around. For example, touch your fingers together and then make them go apart. Stretch out your hands through the palms. Imagine you are looking at your hands for the first time ever.

Practice—
- Turn your hands over, with the backs of your hands facing you.
    - Move the fingers around. For example, spread your fingers apart. Play an imaginary piano, letting your fingers dance across the keys. With the fingers softly

OUR INHERITED WISDOM

curled inward, roll the hands in circles a few times in each direction.
- Make sounds with your hands.
  - Flick the nail of each finger against your thumb. Click your fingers. Clap your hands.
- Hold your hands in different ways.
  - Clasp them. Interlace the fingers. Squeeze them.
- Bring the hands lightly cupped over your nose.
  - Feel your breath on the palms of your hands. Relax your jaw and eyes. Breathe for several breaths.
- Bring your hands over the center of your chest.
  - First, with one hand over the other, take a few breaths and notice the movement in your chest associated with the rhythm of breathing.
  - Then, lightly bring your palms together.
  - Form the shape of a flower bud with your fingertips, and the heels of your palms touching one another.
    - Leave a little space in the center of the palms.
    - Slightly bow your head, pause, and imagine as though the entire world is within that little space between your palms. Stay for a few moments.

Transition Back into Your Day—
- Let your hands relax on your lap. Close your eyes and sit quietly for as long as you like.
- Before you transition back into your day, set an intention to be gentle with your touch.

TOUCH

Divine Awareness and Mind
INNER ATTITUDES

ACCEPTANCE

> Complaint
> is only possible
> while living in the suburbs
> of God.
>
> Hafiz
> *Trans. by Daniel Ladinsky*

As I read the poem by Hafiz, I found myself tempted to complain about complaining. It sometimes seems easier to share a story about a mishap or a mistreatment, or an expected event than to be positive. Fortunately there was a Post-It note on my desk reminding me of "an elm tree."

There was an elm tree that stood for decades in the front yard of my parent's farm on the High Plains in western Kansas. The tree, which had been planted by my father, survived droughts, disease, lightning, gale-force winds, blizzards hail, excessive heat, and ever-changing weather. Yet, it steadily grew without complaint.

As a child, I would rest in the grass in the front yard, watching the elm's leaves dance in the wind and sunlight. Like a trusted friend, that tree always seemed to be there whenever I needed comfort. For example, I appreciated its quiet presence when I sat next to it soon after our beloved dog Poochie died, and later, when our dog Rider died. In my early teens, when

OUR INHERITED WISDOM

my best friend started dating the boy I secretly loved, the elm silently reassured me that life goes on. Outdoor family photos often included some part of the tree, even if only its shadow.

Even after I moved to Europe for a while, the elm tree offered inspiration. When I first attempted a yoga pose named "tree," the elm was there to teach me. Initially, the lesson was just about physical balance, which was extra-challenging because of my inner-pronated feet. The balance on one foot came as I learned to use my own feet with the same stability that my childhood tree-friend had, securely tethered in the earth. The elm's familiar cousins in the form of the wooden floor supported me.

Over the years, more of the elm's limbs died and broke off. Every year for at least ten years, my father would announce, "This is the year" when he would have to cut down "that old elm." In his usual succinct way, his announcement would be short, followed by a pause that invited feedback or comment. Each year, there was a silent message that his commitment had grown stronger, and that we needed to prepare ourselves for the eventuality that the elm really would be cut down.

During that decade, I thought about what it would be like when the elm was gone. I would miss its crusty old bark and graceful presence. I would miss the lopsidedness of its trunk, from having lost some of its limbs in stormy weather. Its trunk had grown wide with age, and seemed to sink more solidly into the ground. In the warm seasons, the leaves that sprouted on its branches still rustled delicately, as though singing to a cloudless blue sky. The elm's branches continued

ACCEPTANCE

to reach upward and outward, as though expressing its eternal beauty and presence.

Whenever I visited the elm, I sat down on a walkway close to this gracious tree. I would trace its shape with my eyes from its base, where the roots sank into the ground, up to its uneven, and increasingly barren, branches. One consistent message was that it was what it was, nothing more and nothing less. The elm was a singular expression of the divine Self. Rather than trying to be the sky, a blade of grass, or any other part of nature, the elm's energy was focused simply on being a tree.

On my last visit with the family elm tree, it had this message: "Sway with the wind, but remain steady. Be still, and feel the raging storms rush over you. Accept the storms and allow a part of yourself to release in return. Listen. All that you need to know is there. Open your arms to the sky as I reach my limbs toward the heavens. Mirror the seasons to the fullest, so that others might share in your splendor. Each season has its beauty. If it is fall, do not mourn springtime. Be a witness to others, as I have been to you. Tolerate and nourish those around you, for they complement your natural brilliance. When your body becomes diseased, remember your true self. For even though I have been stricken with elm disease, I am still the elm that I have always been. Anchor yourself firmly in the universal wisdoms, no matter how rich or sparse they may seem. Be. Just be."

It is now nearly ten years since my father cut down the elm. Even though both the tree and my father are gone, their lessons live on.

OUR INHERITED WISDOM

PRACTICE

This practice supports awareness of being complaint-free.

Prepare—
- Sit on the floor or in a chair. If you are in a chair, place the soles of both feet on the floor.

Practice—
- Rub your palms together vigorously for a few seconds.
  - Then, place your hands lightly over your eyes. Breathe as though you are caressing the breath.
- Rub your palms together again.
  - Then, place your hands over your jaw and the sides of your face. Breathe softly and gently.
- One last time, rub your palms together.
  - Then, place your hands over your heart, one hand on top of the other. Breathe.
- Release your hands to the sides of your body. Sweep your hands and arms upward.
  - Pause for a breath with your hands overhead.
- Bring your palms together overhead.
  - Then, with the palms still together, lower your hands to your heart.
  - Bow your head slightly. Make a vow to be complaint-free.

ACCEPTANCE

Transition Back into Your Day –
- Stay seated.
    - Close your eyes, or have a soft gaze. Sit quietly for several minutes.
- When you are ready, return to your day.

GENTLENESS

*Tenderly, I now touch all
things,
knowing one day we will
part.*

St. John of the Cross
Trans. by Daniel Ladinsky

It is the last new moon of the year. For those of us in the northern hemisphere, this is a moonless night during the darkest period of the year. I find the December new moon a perfect time for reflection. The December darkness is paired with worldwide celebrations of eternal light, and the preparations for a new calendar year. It seems that an invisible hand has reached through the layers of duality and offered tastes of sweetness, generosity, acceptance, compassion, and kindness.

There is also gentleness that seeps into many of our gestures during these final weeks of the year—in hugs, the lighting of candles and lights, gift-giving and other offerings in the spirit of compassion and communion. We may be touched by the deeper meanings of the light within the darkness and feel moved to be more gentle and reverential in our actions. Or, perhaps there is a heightened awareness of the pains and needs of others in the world sparking a desire to share.

OUR INHERITED WISDOM

Gentleness expresses itself in so many ways, and is a gift of the season that we can carry forward as an intention into the New Year. Although it is sometimes considered a weakness, gentleness actually requires an inner strength and awareness.

I've tried basic practices such as being gentle in the way I open and close doors during the day. The doors are symbolic of my connectedness to nature and others through the wood and craftsmanship. Somewhere during the day, a door slams shut. The idiom "gentle as a giant" expresses the need for recognizing our own strength in our words and actions, but also our thoughts. Gentleness inspires us to recognize the fragility of life, taking only what we need, and sharing the rest.

I am in awe of the message from St. John of the Cross, a 16th century saint. In twelve simple words, he conveys his realization of the fragile and fleeting nature of life and our innate power to heal and care from moment to moment. It is easy to imagine his being able to calm and feed even the wildest animal. He embodies the gentleness of one who is peaceful and composed, understanding of imperfections, and through touch, transfers a wish for the best and highest for all. St. John inspires me to continue to explore the quiet way gentleness can reshape my inner attitudes and behaviors.

GENTLENESS

PRACTICE

This practice supports your awareness of gentleness and interconnectedness.

Prepare—
- Shake out your limbs briefly and then come to a seated position.
- Relax through your body.

Practice—
- Breathe -
  - Inhale with a slow, smooth, even in-breath, as though a sweet breeze is caressing your throat and lungs.
  - Exhale with a slow, gentle, even out-breath, as though you are that sweet breeze, nourishing all that is around you.
  - Repeat 3-5 times.
- Keep an even and gentle breath. Face relaxed. Palms upward on your thighs.
- Invite gentleness into your sight, words, thoughts, and hands.
  - *Eyes*—Lightly place your fingertips on your eyelids and invite your lids to soften. Release tension across the surface of your eyes and in the corners.
    - With your hands in your lap, slowly begin to look around at your surroundings. Let your gaze be loving and soft, as though you are observing pure truth and being equally observed in return.

OUR INHERITED WISDOM

- Invite a sense of wonder and amazement of the miraculous beauty of feet, hands and the entire head and body.
  - *Mouth*—Lightly place your fingertips on your lips.
    - Imagine that only loving and caring words will pass through your lips.
  - *Mind*—Lightly place your fingertips on your temples and invite them to relax.
    - Invite loving and caring thoughts.
  - *Hands*—Invite your palms to relax.
    - Imagine pure love is being poured across your palms and fingertips. Pause after the inhale, and imagine that love flows inward toward your heart and that each exhale radiates out through every pore of your being—from head to toe, front to back.
  - Repeat 5-7 times.

Transition Back into Your Day—
- Sit quietly for a few moments before returning to your day.

GENTLENESS

GIVING

I was sad one day and went for a walk;
I sat in a field.

A rabbit noticed my condition and
came near.

It often does not take more than that to help at times–

to just be close to creatures who
are so full of knowing,
so full of love
that they don't
–chat,

they just gaze with
their
marvelous understanding.

St. John of the Cross
Trans. by Daniel Ladinsky

Autumn is approaching in the Northern Hemisphere. The daylight hours are slowly giving way to the longer nights, the squirrels are burying their winter stash, and the deciduous trees are baring their trunks. Even if we miss the cues in nature,

OUR INHERITED WISDOM

nonprofit groups remind us of the arrival of fall with appeals for funds, a new school year has begun, and retail sites are announcing discounts on seasonal products and services.

I feel at the very heart of this season is what I call giving-ness. "Giving-ness," to me, is a state where giving and receiving flow seamlessly. It is what sustains and nourishes us in our daily life. My sense is that, like pure love, this intangible form of giving upholds the world. With each breath, we exchange gifts with the trees. Our food arises through the giving presence of the waters and soil. Symbolically, we give back to the earth through our bodies. The fall equinox offers a momentary balance in the otherwise constant swing between lightness and darkness.

St. John of the Cross and other mystics often use nature as a way to remind us that we abide in giving-ness and that, through it, our fears and sadness can melt into quietude. The rabbit here may be a trickster distracting us and leading us down the rabbit hole away from the awareness of giving-ness. It seems to me that way, because it is easy to overlook the second line, "I sat in a field." In those few, simple words, St. John of the Cross presents the field of spaciousness and stillness to unfold, free of hopping or leaping—just sitting without distraction or expectation.

There, there—there I rest in giving-ness.

GIVING

PRACTICE

This practice symbolically shakes off unwanted emotions and invites lightness into your heart.

Prepare—
- Standing.
- Gently shake one limb at a time, beginning with your right arm. Then, shake your right leg. Then, move to your left side and shake your left arm, and lastly, left leg.
- Shake each limb for at least 30 seconds. If you have an injury, please take care.

Practice—
- Seated.
- Begin by reaching both arms upward and apart.
  - Move slowly, as though you are caressing the space around you.
  - Allow the hands and elbows to be relaxed.
- Then, slowly bring both hands to the center of your chest, with one hand resting over the other.
- Continue this movement and add an awareness of the breath, as follows.
  - Inhale—Slowly allow your hands and arms to move upward into a "v" position.
    - Joints soft. Imagine you are reaching into the darkness.
  - Exhale—Slowly bring your hands over the center of your chest.

OUR INHERITED WISDOM

- Place one hand over the other.
- Imagine you are accepting lightness into your heart.
- Allow a feeling of an inner smile as you receive this gift of light.
  ○ Repeat 5–7 times.

Transition Back into Your Day—
- Sit quietly for a few moments.
- When you are ready, return to your day.

GIVING

LAUGHTER

I could not lie anymore so I started to call my dog "God."
First he looked
confused,

then he started smiling, then he even
danced.

I kept at it: now he doesn't even
bite.

I am wondering if this
might work on
people?

Tukaram
Trans. by Daniel Ladinsky

In the Northern Hemisphere, the daylight hours are slowly growing longer. Buds are beginning to fatten on the tree branches, and migratory birds will soon reappear. Even with the unusual shifts in the weather patterns, it is somehow comforting and uplifting to watch springtime ease back into our lives.

With the brightening of the days, I've been thinking how the shift in seasons is just one of many common experiences. We all have bodies, and need food, air, and water. Viral in-

OUR INHERITED WISDOM

fections touch people of all ages, backgrounds, and classes. We all have the capacity for a wide range of emotions. Stories weave our lives together with ancestors near and far, our environments, and more. And, we are innately susceptible to laughter.

Laughter is one of our most contagious human experiences. It sparks the release of endorphins, which are our natural feel-good chemicals, promoting a sense of overall well-being. It relieves physical tension, boosts the immune system, lifts our mood, and strengthens our capacity to learn new things. There are some studies that suggest that it betters circulation and offers relief from the experience of pain.

The poet Tukaram offers further insight into laughter. He playfully invites us to smile and laugh with the image of a happy and joyful dog. For any of us who have had pets, we know that dogs know when and how to offer comic relief. They are loyal, loving and accepting.

Through a simple story of his dog, Tukaram offers us laughter in the spirit of rejoicing. He allows us to rejoice with him. He reverses the word "dog" to "God" as a reminder that the eternal truth and happiness are found in the simplest moments. If we go chasing after, or away from, true happiness, we will miss it. That is part of the delight in looking in the mirror of our humanness. At the core of our being is childlike, pure joy.

As humans, we have, and have always had, our own direct line to laughter. It comes with a warning to beware that laughter is infectious. When used respectfully, it can make you and others happy; however, if used for malice or at the expense of others, it can bring misery. It is no wonder that my father lived into his nineties. He found reasons to chuckle every day.

LAUGHTER

PRACTICE

This practice supports your awareness of inner joy.

Prepare—
- Sit with your spine in an upright, neutral position. If you are seated in a chair, rest the soles of your feet on the floor.
- Head movements
  - Drop your chin down toward the center of your chest. Pause and smile. Breathe.
  - Lift your chin up toward the ceiling. Pause and smile. Breathe.
  - Tilt your right ear toward your right shoulder. Pause and smile. Breathe.
  - Tilt your left ear toward your left shoulder. Pause and smile. Breathe.

Practice—
- Arm movements
  - Open your palms outward and upward toward the ceiling (your arms will be in a V-shape). Imagine that pure joy is being poured into your palms. Receive that joy in the palms of your hands.
  - Move your arms down and lightly place your palms:
    - On the crown of your head. Imagine the joy is pouring into the spaces between your thoughts.
    - Over the front of your throat, imagining joy seeping into your voice.

OUR INHERITED WISDOM

- Over your heart, imagining pure joy rushing into your heart center.
  - Each area, smile and breathe 2-3 breaths.
  - Let your hands rest in your lap. Imagine every cell in your body is joyful. With slightly upturned corners of your lips, bathe in that joy.

Transition Back into Your Day—
- Sweep your palms and arms upward and outward. Turn the face slightly upward.
  - Imagine that you are overflowing with joy and sharing the abundance with the universe.
  - Smile and breathe.
  - Perhaps laugh with the joy of being alive.
- Transition back into your day when you are ready.

LAUGHTER

REVERENCE

I ask all blessings,
I ask them with reverence,
of my mother the earth,
of the sky, moon, and sun my father.

Navajo Wisdom

The air was moist and still. Given the weather earlier in the day, I had expected a breeze, along with the rustle of fall leaves and the creak of branches in the wind. But, this September eve was quiet.

I felt enveloped in the soft and peaceful darkness. It seemed as though everything had been tucked under a large, magical blanket.

With a dense cloud covering, the horizon had disappeared, along with any sense of separateness between heaven and earth. There was barely a visible trace of the houses, trees, and the rest of my neighborhood surroundings. No pets or wildlife stirred. With the expansive quiet, even my mind relaxed away from its usual running monologue about the outer happenings. It was just the universe, cradling all its life forms in the eternal pulse of life.

A reddish ember caught my eye. Given the number of wildfires that have happened close to the area where I live in California, I noticed a tinge of fear arise in me. It was an irrational fear, since the brightness was high in the night sky,

OUR INHERITED WISDOM

far from where I stood. Still, the glistening was a sweet reminder of how nature and all her beauty can shine a light on the innerscape. Such beauty can spark a sense of reverent joy, simply for the gift of being alive.

As I read these words from a member of the Navajo Nation, I am feeling blessed to have them cross my path. They are likely not a perfect or complete translation, but they convey a timeless message that we, as humans, are part of an intricate, larger web of life, spinning in the sky.

I feel that the indigenous and ancient people are wise guides. Their words gently remind us that the earth, sky, and other life forms do not exist solely for humans. They anonymously mapped the stars so that we could navigate through life, revealed the healing qualities of plants, and recognized our capacity both to destroy and protect life. They created universal values such as truthfulness and non-greed, and living with reverence.

REVERENCE

PRACTICE

This practice supports awareness of reverence within everyday life.

Prepare—
- Gently close your eyes. Imagine that you can release any tension in your eyelids and your eyeballs. Slowly move your eyes up to down, left to right, and then diagonally (first, upper right to lower left, and, then upper left to lower right).

Practice—
- Open your eyes with a soft gaze.
    - Slowly let your eyes scan around the room or area where you are.
    - Allow your eyes to rest on the floor or ground beneath you. Then slowly shift your gaze to a few other spots.
    - As your rest your eyes in a particular spot, notice the textures, colors, etc., without judgment.
- Return your gaze to the first spot.
    - If you are indoors, let your mind take note of the source of the materials.
        - For example, a natural wood floor would come from trees. A concrete floor would likely come from sand that has been ground and mixed with water.
        - Imagine the sources, as though your true self resides here instead of in your thoughts.
    - Wherever you are, silently acknowledge the gift of the space around you.

OUR INHERITED WISDOM

- Then, lightly close your eyes and sit quietly for a few moments with a feeling of great reverence for life. (Please feel free to keep your eyes open, if that is more comfortable for you.)

Transition Back into Your Day—
- Continue to sit quietly for a few moments.
- Breathe.
  - Notice the gentle rise and release of your breath.
  - Acknowledge the gift of breath as an ever-present reminder of your constant link to all of life.
- When you are ready, return to your day.

REVERENCE

SPACIOUSNESS

Out beyond ideas of wrongdoing and rightdoing,
there is a field. I'll meet you there.
When the soul lies down in that grass,
the world is too full to talk about.
Ideas, language, even the phrase each other
doesn't make any sense.

Rumi
Trans. by Coleman Barks

As the season changes to spring in the northern hemisphere, it feels as though nature is inviting us to begin anew. As the days are grow longer, migratory birds reappear along with insects, such as butterflies and bees. Fresh leaves are unfurling on the trees, tulips and daffodils are forming buds, and mountain creeks have reappeared.

The springtime meadows and fields are wide expanses of green. I have many memories associated with fields as the new growth emerges. My earliest ones are from my childhood, when I would ride with my dad to look at his fields. I could barely see out of the pickup window, but was captivated by the immensity of the flat Kansas horizon and vastness of the blue sky and green land. More recent memories are from hikes with my husband Jay to large meadows in the wilderness.

OUR INHERITED WISDOM

These memories carry a sense of spaciousness, peacefulness and the promise of eternal abundance. To me, open spaces are both symbolic and physical reminders of the essence of our humanness. On a practical level, they are the sources of the plants that nourish our bodies. Regardless of our dietary preferences, plants form the foundation of nearly all of the worlds' foods.

Symbolically, we can rest our minds and hearts in the boundless openness. There, there is only pure awareness. It has no purpose other than to nourish the soul of all. It is ever abundant, eternally free and open. In the world, it sprouts seeds of kindness, equanimity, gentleness, and compassion. These are rooted in the universality of truthfulness, non-harming, and non-greed.

The springtime fields can remind us of how to be authentically "human." The word human, as with humility, derives from the Latin word, *humus,* earth. The earth itself is nourished and fertilized by the changing of seasons. Leaves from last year's trees are nutrients for renewal. As we let go of old paradigms and habits, new growth can occur. I believe that we once again can remember that we are connected to all life through our breath and food, and through the enduring field of divine love.

SPACIOUSNESS

PRACTICE

This practice brings awareness to subtle, inner qualities, such as compassion and humility.

Prepare—
- Find a comfortable seated position. If seated in a chair, place both feet on the floor.
    - Take a moment and vigorously shake out your arms. Imagine as though you are letting go of habits of gossip, judgment, and finding fault with others.
    - When you feel complete, let your hands relax in your lap.
    - Stretch your mouth wide, and make an imaginary yell from deep in your belly.
        - Imagine as though you are clearing out any debris of insecurity, lack of confidence or clinging to scarcity.
    - Relax your mouth.
        - Take a few deeper breaths.

Practice—
- Place your hands over your heart.
- Choose one of the following qualities that you would like to grow within your newly cleansed inner field: kindness, equanimity, gentleness, or compassion.
    - Breathe naturally.
    - Silently, lovingly, and slowly repeat the quality your have chosen.

OUR INHERITED WISDOM

- Feel as though that every cell in your mind and body is longing for, and soaking up, that quality. Particularly pay attention to the palms of your hands, the center of your head, and your mouth—the areas of your thoughts, words, and actions.
- Let your entire being be infused with that sense that you are that quality.

Transition Back into Your Day—
- Slowly stretch your hands and arms outward and upward.
- Bring your palms lightly together over your head. Then, with the palms still together, lower them to the front of your heart in a prayer position.
- Nod your head downward toward your heart and, with a sense of humility, offer gratitude for your capacity to let go of old habits and embrace new qualities for the well-being of all.
  - If you have a particular faith, please adjust this prayerful gesture according to your belief.
- When you are ready, return to your day.

SPACIOUSNESS

THANKFULNESS

Without You — my Life, my Love —
I would never have wandered across these endless
   countries.
You have poured out so much grace for me,
Done me so many favors, given me so many gifts—
I look everywhere for Your love—
Then suddenly I am filled with it.

Rābi'a
Trans. by Charles Upton

The farmers' market was busy. As I stood in line at a vegetable stand, I repeatedly heard the words "Thank you." Besides those who were exchanging money for their basketful of produce, there were others asking one another about particular vegetables—what they were, and how to prepare them. There was the utterance of thanks at the end of each conversation.

It seems so easy to express thankfulness, yet truly difficult to absorb the depth and richness within the moment of thanks. For example, one ear of corn at the farmers' market has not only been handled and tended by many hands, but it is a composite of the elements. It embodies the nutrients and moisture of the soil, the rain and sunshine from the sky, and the winds that help in pollination. When dried, it adorns tables and serves as decorations for fall festivities. And, when

OUR INHERITED WISDOM

featured in ancient legends, it represents the infinite interconnection between humans, heaven, and all of life.

I feel that to hold a head of lettuce, an ear of corn, or any plant or non-plant form is to hold a mini-version of the world in our hands. This would include all the mass-produced and handmade items that fill our homes and lives. A piece of chocolate or even clothing has likely been fabricated and shipped thousands of miles, using electricity, and fossil fuel, along with the work of other humans. Like us, they rely on the gifts of the earth—the air, the trees that make the air breathable, drinkable water, arable soil, food and shelter, and a network of other humans who have taught, raised, and hopefully loved, them.

Rābi'a seems to offer a sweet nudge to be sincere every time we express thanks. When we foster sincere thankfulness, reverence and acceptance will quietly bloom within us—acceptance, in the sense that in order to truly give thanks, we first need to fully receive the gifts we have and are given. As we release and let go, we realize that our earthly existence is a dynamic play of love in every aspect of life. Eventually, like Rābi'a, we become love itself.

Despite our world's incredible losses, violence, and tragedies, Rābi'a and other great saints, prophets, and sages offer prayerful hope for all of humanity to remember the grace of life within each moment. Every flower, ear of corn, cloud, or smile is a doorway to see more than what is on the surface. A simple pause, such as being at a farmers' market, is an opening to step out of habitual words and to shift our inner lens toward reverent thankfulness, so that we can move,

THANKFULNESS

consume, speak, and act with more clarity and care. If more and more of us do this, then perhaps we will lighten the hearts of others.

PRACTICE

This practice supports your awareness of reciprocity.

Prepare—
- Begin standing.
  - Gently shake out each of your limbs.
  - Move freely around the room, as though dancing to your own inner tune. (Note: this will vary from day to day)

Practice—
- Still standing.
- Reach your arms toward the sky. Turn your face upward. Imagine that you are being showered with blessings.
  - Arms go back along your sides. Take a few easy breaths.
- Reach your arms out to your sides, palms upward.
  - Slowly turn 360°. Imagine you are touching an infinite amount of abundance.
    - If inside, imagine that every wall and object is filled

OUR INHERITED WISDOM

  with gifts from the earthly elements and other people, including your ancestors.
    - If outside, imagine that everything around you is a gift—the trees, plants, sky, animals, insects, etc.
  - Arms go back along your sides. Take a few easy breaths.
- Reach your arms toward the floor. If your back is okay, bend forward, with your fingertips toward your feet, as you do this.
  - Imagine that you are standing upon all past and future generations.
  - Arms go back along your sides. Take a few easy breaths.

Transition Back into Your Day—
- Come to a seated position.
  - If on a chair, place the soles of both feet on the floor. If seated on the floor, place support under your hips.
  - Find a gentle lift through your spine. Soften your facial expression. Perhaps bring a gentle smile to your face.
  - Bring your palms over your heart, one hand on top of the other.
- Imagine you are filled with an abundance of gifts from all directions—above, to the sides, and below. Invite a sense of reverent awe and appreciation that you are a composite of all these gifts.
  - With each in-breath, imagine that the breath is

THANKFULNESS

radiating out from the center of your heart and carrying these gifts to the surface of your body.
  - With each out-breath, imagine that you are truly accepting/receiving these gifts into the deepest core of your being.
- Take a minimum of three breaths this way.
- Release your palms onto your lap, palms upward. If you wish, close your eyes.
- Sit quietly until you are ready to return to your day.

Divine Freedom
SKY AND LIGHT

CELESTIAL LIGHT

Like a great starving beast
My body is quivering
Fixed
On the scent
Of
Light.

Hafiz
Trans. by Daniel Ladinsky

It seems fanciful that a new moon can appear to shimmer. Yet, about once every eighteen months, there is a radiant glow around a new moon. It occurs when the two orbs of the moon and the sun seem to mate in the daytime sky, and the moon has cloaked the sun.

I admire the odd and wondrous relationship between this unlikely pair. They couldn't be more different in their natures. The moon is tiny and constantly mobile, whereas the sun is massive—about four hundred times larger than the moon—and ever-steady and luminous. Still, they have an intimate interconnection, and model balance and altruism with their unique and vast differences.

The sun, in spite of its center-stage prominence in the solar system, freely offers warmth and light to all. In some cultures and religions, the sun's radiance is an archetype of

OUR INHERITED WISDOM

the immortal, supreme light and love that holds life. And, the moon is its partner, reflecting light into the darkness. It helps stabilize the earth's rotation and regulate our tides. Together, they provide us with energy, illumination, inspiration, and our calendar.

Ancients recognized the magnificent power and significance of these two spherical bodies. Nowadays, we need a cosmic jolt to renew the awe of our raw link to them and the rest of life. When the dark moon covers the sun, it is like a power outage, especially in the locations where an eclipse will be visible.

For days, and some human lore says for months, things can be turned upside-down before and after a solar eclipse. There can be distressing energies, turbulence, and waves of negativity and misfortune. Plants, animals, humans and the elements can be affected. The change in the gravitational pull may cause earthquakes and other terrestrial phenomena. We may feel forced to leap into the new. Still, all is not gloomy; near the totality of the eclipse, the sun reveals its brightness and presence by giving the moon a glimmering appearance.

Poets like Hafiz remind us that light is always there. It will always illumine us, even if we ignore or forget about it, or when we think it has abandoned us in our bleakness. Like the moon, we have the capacity to reflect or eclipse the light, with the former the more normal way of being and the latter, temporary and occasional.

We can either look upward or downward to the glow, to the heavens or to cyber messages. Both can take us inward and both impact how we interact outward. For my guidance,

CELESTIAL LIGHT

I choose the more mysterious glow that shines in everyone and in all aspects of life.

PRACTICE

This practice supports awareness of your inner light.

Prepare—
- *Invite quietude*—Turn your phone to airplane mode and put it aside.
  - Remove items from your wrists, such as your watch or any non-medical monitor.
    - However, if you know you only have a set amount of time, please feel free to use an alarm.
- *Sit comfortably*—Come to a seated position, either in a chair or on the floor, where your spine is effortlessly upright.
  - If seated in a chair, place the soles of your feet on the floor. If your feet don't reach the floor, please place a cushion or a block under them.
- *Relax your hands*—Give a gentle squeeze to each hand by placing the thumb of the opposite hand on the palm and wrapping the other fingers over the back of the hand, and squeeze.

OUR INHERITED WISDOM

  ○ Then, let the hands relax on your lap in any position that is comfortable.
- *Relax your eyes and face*—Either close your eyelids or have them open. If open, let your eyes rest in a soft, gentle gaze. Relax your forehead, jaw, and chin.

Practice—
- Imagine a steady, radiant glow of light similar to that of the early morning or late day sun. Imagine that with that light, there is an overwhelming presence of well-being, protection, and love.
- Sequentially, imagine that
  - the building that you are in is infused with light—every wall, ceiling, floor, window, and door, as well as the roof and foundation.
  - the room you are in is made of light.
  - the cushion or chair that you are seated on is made of light.
  - you are bathed and enfolded in light.
  - you are luminous…you are the steady, radiant glow of light.
  - there is only light.
    - Note: You may wish to open your eyes, silently read a line, e.g., "the building…," and then sit quietly imagining that layer before moving to the next line.
    - Follow your pace of awareness. Savor the light.

CELESTIAL LIGHT

Transition Back into Your Day—
- If your eyes were closed, slowly open them.
- Allow the awareness of your breath to seep in. Notice the gentle movement of the chest and ribs associated with the breath.
- After several breaths, slowly lower your chin to your chest and rock your head from side to side in half-circles. Shrug through your shoulders. Stretch through your palms and squeeze your hands. Before standing up, stretch through your toes and feet.
- When you are ready, return to your day.

CLOUDS

Observe your life, between two breaths.
Breath is a wind, both coming and going.
On this wind you have built your life–
but how will a castle rest on a cloud?

Avicenna
Trans. by David Fideler and Sabrineh Fideler

Skyscrapers appeared in the distance. At least what looked like the outline of a city skyline. Yet, it was simply towers of clouds outside the airplane window. I was lucky enough to have seatmates who were fine with our window shade open, so I could watch the passing skyscape-shaped clouds. My mind was joyously entertained as we soared through the clouds. I watched as the first "city" disappeared, followed by several others.

    For me, clouds are easy and fun to observe. I grew up where the prominent view was the sky. The horizon was nearly free of buildings, trees, or even rises in the earth. Rather than just being visible overhead, clouds there are often in direct eyesight near the flat horizon. On any given day in my childhood, animal-shaped clouds raced across the sky, clouds of mountains and forests arose, and sailboats and horses in the form of clouds took me anywhere I wanted to go.

    It is no wonder that in various religious and spiritual

OUR INHERITED WISDOM

traditions, clouds are symbols of our thoughts and emotions. They are transient, often move quickly, and are ever-changing. Their shapes and characteristics reflect the nature of the atmospheric state: calm, hazy, or stormy.

A seemingly weightless *cumulus* (from Latin for "heap") cloud—one that looks like heaps of cotton—can weigh over a million pounds. A thundercloud can weigh over a billion pounds! Clouds are formed and moved by basic matter, such as air, water and the dust of the earth.

Wise beings around the world, such as the poet Avicenna, inspire us to remember that rather than the clouds, our true nature is akin to their backdrop—the sky. Yet, that isn't immediately perceptible in the midst of the ever-changing sensory delights of daily life. With all the enchanting sights, smells, textures, and sounds, our thoughts follow their own cloud-like nature.

It takes a peek beneath the surface of our thoughts to discover our unending, sweet self. At our very heart, we are peaceful, clear, kind, and loving. While I might enjoy the patterns of my thoughts, I try to let them slide by, like clouds in the wind.

CLOUDS

PRACTICE

This practice supports awareness of peacefulness beneath the changing clouds of the mind.

Prepare—
- Sit quietly for a few moments.

Practice (early morning) –
- Standing
- Put your palms over the center of your chest.
  - Notice the feeling of your hands touching one another, and touching this symbolic spiritual heart center.
  - Imagine that infinite, expansive peace and joy reside here, rather than your thoughts.
    - If you have a particular religion or spiritual practice, imagine that which you hold as most supreme resides in your heart.
- For five cycles, sync your breath with the movement.
  - Begin—Pause, with your arms at your sides.
  - Inhale—Reach your palms forward and upward.
    - Pause for one to two seconds at the end of your inhale and before the exhale (with your arms overhead). Soften and relax, as though you are completely releasing any un-needed tension.
  - Exhale—With palms together, move them down the centerline of your face and upper chest to your heart center.

OUR INHERITED WISDOM

- Pause for one to two seconds at the end of your exhale, and before you inhale (with your palms over your heart center). Soften and relax, recalling the loving peace that is ever-present.

Transition Back into Your Day—
- Sit quietly, your palms resting over your heart center.
- For five, easy cycles of breath, pause briefly between inhalation and exhalation.
  - Imagine your breath beginning at the center of your heart.
    - Inhale—Imagine loving peace radiating outward from your heart to the surface of your body.
    - Exhale—Imagine loving peace flowing back into your heart center and into the depths of your heart.
  - Then, if you have time, sit quietly, your palms resting on your thighs.

CLOUDS

DAWN

Night is passing,
sun comes by dawn,
Awaken now, beauty's essence,
heart of love.

Hakim Omar Khyyám
Trans. by Nahid Angha, Ph.D.

As the new year began, I reflected on the people I know who had lost someone special recently. Funerals and services have been held for daughters, mothers, wives, husbands, sons, fathers, sisters, and brothers. Some deaths were sudden and unexpected, and some came after a long struggle with illness. Yet, each death brought about grief and sorrow, which the survivors are each quietly traversing in their own way.

While the calendar gives a sharp demarcation between the past and the future year—between December 31 and January 1—these recent losses seemed to be a reminder of the more nuanced relationships of endings and beginnings. As humans, we need time and a sense of past and future to anchor us within our ever-changing lives.

Nature has her own way of offering us comfort and strength. We rely on the regularity of the patterns of the sun and the moon. Each morning, the sun appears on the horizon, awakening the day. Like a sweet mother, she rouses everyone and sets them in motion toward their life activities. At first

OUR INHERITED WISDOM

light, diurnal creatures begin to stir, birds sing, roosters crow, dogs bark, and eventually the din of vehicles and mechanical beeps arrives.

A primal part of us senses the magnificence of the daily arrival of the sun. The sun nourishes us not only through the growth of plants for our food, but through its light and vital energy. Different studies have shown that exposure to sunlight can reduce anxiety and calm the nerves. It stimulates inner systems, such as the metabolism of minerals, and helps glands that take care of internal secretion. It is considered the natural source of Vitamin D connected to the production of the hormone endorphin, which gives us the feelings of satisfaction and happiness.

Not surprisingly, ancient sages viewed the dawn as symbolic of hope, the end of the shadows of pain and hardship, and the promise of renewal. The parade of colors across the sky surpasses even the greatest of human inventions and evokes a raw awareness of the powerful essence of life. We somehow recognize that within this one dawn are all the many dawns that have come before and that will come afterward. Splendid, glorious beauty glimmers in the morning light and lovingly charms the sun to shine anew.

This dawning of the day inspires the deepest part of us—our inner sun—to rise into, and be held in the loving embrace of, the divine. Through the simple language of nature, the poet Hakim Omar Khyyám offers praise to the sanctity of life that is held in a peaceful balance between life and death, night and day.

DAWN

PRACTICE

This practice supports the awareness of gift of dawn.

Prepare—
- Sit in a comfortable position, either on a chair, or on the floor.
- Stretch your hands and arms out to the sides. Stretch through the center of your palms to your fingertips.
- Cross your arms over the front of your body and give yourself a big hug.
- Allow your hands to rest in your lap. Let yourself release tension—physically, mentally, and emotionally.

Practice—
- Reach your arms upward and slightly outward, as though into the expanse of the sky. Then, allow your hands to return to your lap.
    - Close your eyes, if that is comfortable. Otherwise, keep them in a soft, somewhat inward gaze.
- Imagine you are lovingly surrounded and enfolded by the beauty of the early morning light. Allow the gentle glow to absorb current worries or fears.
- Quietly shift your attention to the quality of your inhalation and exhalation.
    - Invite the transitions between the in-and-out-breaths to be smooth, even, and quiet.
- Allow the feeling that your breath is infused with the soft radiance of dawn.
    - Imagine that each cell, each atom of your being, is silently uttering, "Love. Peace. Joy."
    - Gently allow these utterances to melt any deep

OUR INHERITED WISDOM

- tightening of the muscles around your heart, sternum, back ribs, belly, neck and shoulder area, face and skull.
  - For as long as is comfortable, allow yourself to receive the abundant awareness of love, peace, and joy, ebbing and flowing. Let its presence hold you, like a cradle stretched between night and day.
- Still attentive to your breath, smile and stretch your palms outward in gratitude for the awareness of the light of love. If your eyes were closed, open them into a soft gaze.

Transition Back into Your Day—
- Sit quietly for a few minutes. Observe your surroundings. Imagine each item that had joined you over the last few moments was now glimmering with love, peace, and joy.
- When you are ready, return to your day.

DAWN

GRACE OF LIGHT

Cut brambles long enough,
Sprout after sprout,
And the lotus will bloom
Of its own accord:
Already waiting in the clearing,
The single image of light.
The day you see this,
That day you will become it.

Sun Bu-er
Trans. by Thomas Cleary

As I climbed the steps to our home, I felt as though some small daisy-like flowers were greeting me. Their heads were turned toward the stairs, as if to welcome everyone with brightness and joy.

Even though I had overloaded myself by trying to carry everything from the car in one trip, I paused to marvel at the flowers' fragile petals radiating perfectly from their centers. They had been small buds just a few days earlier, but now were in full bloom. Here they were, facing the possibility of being eaten by the deer at any moment, yet they kept growing, fully utilizing the support of every drop of water, nutrient in the soil, and ray from the sun.

My heart felt lightened. These sweet flowers had reminded me of a simple lesson. Illumination is needed to help us see—for both inner and outer sight. The name daisy comes from the Anglo-Saxon "daes eage," or "day's eye," indicating how the florets open to sunshine and close to cloudiness or night.

Light sparks life. As sunlight, it nourishes the plants, which in turn nourish humans and other beings. In cartoons and drawings, ideas are represented with light bulbs. Even a small amount of light can dispel confusion and inspire insight. On a deeper level, light is associated with resilience, clarity, softness and gentleness, healing, peace, happiness, truth, love, wisdom, and light-heartedness.

Almost universally, religions and cultures celebrate light as symbolic of everlasting truth and love. Divine light is an unseen, loving presence that melts the boundaries of separateness.

When our awareness is infused with the light beyond all light, compassion and kindness become our natural way of being. We lose our sense of separateness, and our judgmental and destructive tendencies disappear into lightness. We realize the radiant oneness in all.

GRACE OF LIGHT

PRACTICE

This short practice supports awareness of the grace of light.

Prepare—
- Lightly shake out each of your limbs. Then, gently stretch.
- Sit in a comfortable seated position.
  - If you are in a chair, please place the soles of your feet on the floor.
- Invite relaxation into your face, shoulders, and hands. Allow your belly to relax and your breath to be soft and easy.

Practice—
- Still seated, reach your arms out to your sides.
  - Imagine they are rays of your inner light stretching outward. If comfortable for your shoulders, stretch your arms in a V-position, then alongside your ears and back down toward your lap.
- Gently raise your hands upward. Open the palms in front of your chest as though you were ready to gather water from a running faucet.
  - Hold your palms open and imagine a soft, gentle light flowing into your palms.
  - Gather the light and sweep your palms lightly over your face.
  - Then, continue to gather the light and softly bathe yourself in light.
    - This can be a few broad strokes, e.g., down your

OUR INHERITED WISDOM

    arms and legs, and across the front of your throat and torso.
- Relax your hands into your lap, palms in any position that is comfortable.
  - Sit quietly, still softly inhaling and exhaling.
    - Your eyes can be closed or in a soft gaze.
  - Invite the feeling that every cell in your body and face is lightly smiling.
- Once you feel complete, invite a sense that you are glowing from the inside out.

Transition Back into Your Day—
- Take a few deep breaths.
- Stretch in any way that feels natural.
- Open your mouth wide and move your jaw around.
- Smile. Stretch again.
- When you are ready, return to your day, full of the grace of light.

GRACE OF LIGHT

LUMINOUS NATURE

Even if I
repeated love's name
forever,
could outward life match
the intensity of our hearts?

Izumi Shikubu
Trans. by Jane Hirshfield

I was walking at a beach north of San Francisco this morning, and the tide was unusually high. A ranger said it was due to the moon's swinging nearer to the earth than it has in 68 years, and, therefore, the moon's gravity was pulling harder on the oceans.

The beach looked like a bed of a restless sleeper. The sand formed mini-canyons and drop-offs; logs were strewn about. Instead of the rhythmic whisper of the waves, there was a churning roar. Gulls huddled in groups far from the shore.

With such a chaotic scene, I couldn't help but wonder whether this close, bright full moon would have a similar effect on our emotional landscape. Whether it does or not, life itself tugs us between the ends of the spectrum of emotions—from elation to sorrow; turmoil to peace; attraction to repulsion; doubt to trust; humility to pride; and endless hopes, desires and fear.

OUR INHERITED WISDOM

Each of us has our own personal life journey of ups and downs. Yet, ancient sages and saints remind us that our true essence is unwavering. They remind us our true self is not the emotional and mental shifts caused by outer experience. Beneath the appearance of change is a steady, luminous core brimming with love and compassion for all of life. The ancients called this core "heart," and symbolically placed it at the center of our chest. (The anatomical heart had not yet been defined.)

This poem by the 11th century poet Shikubu reminds me of the ancient teachings on the vastness of the heart. The heart has absolute understanding. It knows the nature of all existence, from the smallest atom to the expanse of the galaxies, and knows consciousness beyond words, time and space. In the light of true knowledge, this ever-present core glows with intense brilliance and overflows with insight and clarity.

We have outward reminders of brightness of the heart in nature, such as the sun and the moon's reflection of the sun. There are common gestures in daily life. We bring our hands together in prayer in front of the heart. When asked to point to ourselves, we normally point to the heart center, not to our head. Intuitively, we know that "the heart knows all," and it can be our steady guide through the phases and sways of life.

LUMINOUS NATURE

PRACTICE

This practice supports awareness of your luminous nature.

Prepare—
- Sit in a comfortable position.
- If you wear glasses, remove them for this first part of the practice.
- Vigorously rub your hands together until you feel some warmth in your palms.
- Close your eyes and lightly place the heels of your palms over your eyelids.
    - Stay there for a few breaths until you feel your eyes relax.
    - Then, lightly brush your fingertips in circles around the eyes twice, i.e., move your fingers up to the forehead, down along the temples and under the eyes to the outer edges of the nose, and up to the forehead again.
- Relax—Let your hands rest comfortably on your thighs. Without forcing, breathe in and out with a slow, even breath.

Practice—
- Imagine the brilliant light of the full moon glowing above you.
    - Then, imagine that luminosity seeping in through your closed eyelids and pouring into your heart. Let the light come to rest in the deepest core of the heart.

OUR INHERITED WISDOM

- Quietly breathe.
  - Let your mind settle into the soft, radiant warmth, light, and expanse of your heart.
    - Your mind may rebel. If so, reassure your mind that it isn't forgotten, and that for now, it can rest.
    - Imagine that your eyes and ears are also settling into the embrace of the light in your heart.
- Continue to quietly breathe, letting your entire being be bathed in the light. Just be. Stay for as long as the focus on remains steady and easeful.

Transition Back into Your Day—
- Slowly and gently, place one hand over your heart. Gently place your other hand on top of the first hand.
- Stay in place, with your hands over your heart for a few moments, until you are ready to return to your day.

LUMINOUS NATURE

PRE-DAWN

Keep walking, though there is no place to get to.
Don't try to see through the distances.
That's not for human beings.   Move within,
but don't move in the way fear makes you move.

Rumi
Trans. by Coleman Barks

There was a loud snap outside our front door. It was early morning and the world was yet to stir—that is, most of world. Some other being was also up and moving around. I paused for a few seconds and listened. My ears were greeted by peaceful silence and I felt myself slip into inner quietude.

If there is any time that I feel at home, it is pre-dawn. These early twilight hours feel open and expansive like endless horizon of the Great Plains where I grew up. It is as though there is fullness posing as nothingness. On the surface, it seems as though nothing is happening—no birds are singing, no traffic, no smells of coffee—but yet, the mystical beauty and potentiality of all life is there.

As the tranquility slipped into the background, I could feel my senses come alive. My nose registered the scent of jasmine and my eyes the emerging daylight. There was the faint outline of two shapes hidden in the trees near our front steps. In the early light, the forms were barely discernable.

OUR INHERITED WISDOM

Two deer—a mother and fawn—were grazing the wild grasses. Their translucent presence gave the appearance that they were otherworldly beings in earthly form. In the lore of mythology, deer are considered to be messengers of grace, serenity, gentleness and innocence. They convey the qualities for navigating difficult and unpredictable terrain with calmness, lightness, and acuity. Instead of living in fear, they swiftly move away. They are revered in stories for being able to hear the wordless wisdom of great teachers and for melting the hearts of demons with their loving gaze.

Divine messages are everywhere. They are tucked in the cycles, rhythms, and countless beings of nature. They invite us to harmonize our minds and hearts with our planetary existence and responsibilities, all with loving humility. I feel that to "move within," as Rumi proposes, is to embrace, and live by, our finer, subtler qualities written in the language of the planet and cosmos. This language is echoed in the words of sages, saints, prophets, and wise poets.

The quietude of pre-dawn and the deer can open us to discovering the rich reservoir of gifts that reside within and all around us. I feel the first step is to fully reconnect with the net of reverence for all life.

PRE-DAWN

PRACTICE

This practice supports awareness of pre-sleep habits in preparation for the following dawn.

Prepare—
- Choose an evening when you feel you can attempt to be cyber-free for one hour before bedtime.

Practice—
- One hour before you plan to get into bed, minimize the potential influences on your mind.
  - Drink only tap water or herbal tea.
  - Disconnect, i.e., from your phone, computer, television, tablets, e-readers, and all digital devices.
  - Limit reading any material related to politics, war, self-improvement, society or famous people, or work-related material, e.g., books, papers or magazines.
  - Note how this this feels.
- During that "free" hour:
  - Take extra time with your nighttime habits, e.g., brushing your teeth.
  - Look around your sleeping space.
    - Ideally, move all electronics at least five feet from where you rest your head at night, and out of reach of your hands. Try using a non-electronic alarm clock.

- Lightly touch–
    - The things you have chosen to have near you during your sleep.
    - Your bedding and pillows.
    - Imagine that all these things are your friends.
        - Allow yourself to feel genuinely grateful for these friends.

Transition into Your Sleep—
- Either before you get into bed, or when you first get into bed
    - Take one of your hands to your heart.
    - Consider beneficial qualities you really value in yourself, e.g., gentleness, light-heartedness,
    - Choose one as your intention for the next day.
    - Take ten easy, breaths.
        - Say to yourself—"Now, "I breathe in"; and, "Now, I breathe out."
- Sweet dreams.

PRE-DAWN

SUN-RISE

He who binds to himself a joy
Does the winged life destroy.
But he who kisses the joy as it flies
Lives in eternity's sun rise.

William Blake

As the sun appeared on the horizon, the darkness of the night began to slip away. The aroma of moist soil wafted through the open window, signaling that the rain had ceased. It was a serene, beautiful, and graceful transition from night to day.

I could not help but revel in joy. If I were a bird, I would have swept across the sky, singing a refrain of praise. I would alight on a tree and let it caress my feet with one of its skyward branches. Then, I would stretch my wings as if to tickle the space that holds the tree and all the other beings as our earthly home hurtles around its axis—at the equator, the earth rotates at about a thousand miles per hour.

From the winged perspective, everything is an expression of joy. No one can own it, yet it is a secret ingredient of life. The closest we can come to knowing joy is within each breath. Like wings, the breath rises and falls, gives and takes, receives and offers, and seamlessly floats through the air. If we are upset, clingy, fearful, or greedy, the breath is stressed almost as though its wings are broken. If we are genuinely free, the breath soars.

OUR INHERITED WISDOM

As an embodied being, I am in awe of how Nature consistently wakes us up each day. Like a mother, she nudges us to see the eternal Absolute, represented by the sun. She inspires us with the beauty of flowers, mountains, and hillsides. She possesses all the jewels—gems, ores, water, air, etc.—yet shares them freely. She nourishes us, even though we ignore her and try to conquer her with our own inventions.

With each sunrise, I hope to remember to cherish the precious gift of being a living, breathing being and an integral part of the living, breathing earth. I will endeavor to remember as my father always reminded me, "We are given breath when we come into this world and release it when we leave. It is up to us each day to do the best we can and know that all of life is on loan."

As Blake reminds us, within each moment there is a "sun" "rise:" the constancy of the sun, and the continual movement of the earth that reveals—or lets us see the rise of—the sun each day. The horizon lets us enter into the *forever* and *ever*.

SUN-RISE

PRACTICE

This practice brings awareness of how our moods influence the breath.

Prepare—
- Seated or standing.
- Simply notice your breath.
  - Notice the movement in the ribs, shoulders, arms, and torso associated with your breath.
  - Then, notice the rhythm of your breath.

Practice—
- Between each of the following practices, take a moment to stretch out your hands and arms. Take four-to-five deep breaths. Then, shake out your arms and smile. Within each practice, notice what happens to the ease of the breath. (Note: The first several practices emulate bodily expressions of stressful emotions. If you are already feeling tense you might want to skip to the sixth line.)
  - Scrunch up your face tightly. Notice your breath.
  - Glare, as though looking at your phone or a screen. Notice your breath.
  - Frown, as though concentrating deeply. Notice your breath.
  - Slump your shoulders and let your head hang forward. Notice your breath.
  - Make tight fists and squeeze all the muscles in your arms. Notice your breath.

OUR INHERITED WISDOM

- Observe something beautiful around you, such as a flower. Notice your breath.
- If you have a view of nature, rest your eyes on a tree or another part of nature. Notice your breath.
- Smile, as though smiling from your heart. Notice your breath.
- Touch your fingers lightly to your lips, kiss your fingers, and then release the kiss into the air by moving your hands outward and upward toward the sky. Notice your breath.
- Release any unneeded tension in your shoulders and hands. Notice your breath.

Transition Back into Your Day—
- Take a few moments to sit quietly with your eyes closed or open (in a soft gaze). Let your hands rest comfortably in your lap.
- As you are ready, transition back into your day.

SUN-RISE

Divine Freedom
PAUSE, STILLNESS AND SOLITUDE

EARTH

Touched by all that love is
I draw closer to you
Saddened by all that love is
I run from you

Surprised by all that love is
I remain alert in stillness

František Halas

Having grown up on a farm, I maintain a childlike amazement at the natural world. Within the period of an hour, an overcast sky clears, baring a blue expanse. A fawn, still with spots on its back, wanders across the hillside near the kitchen window. The mother trails behind. A heart-shaped stone appears on a pathway that I have traversed dozens of times.

Awe feels like a natural state of being. I close my eyes, and it is there. I open my eyes, and the world appears as a composite of whirling miracles sustaining the whole. If my amazement drops away, a hearty clover sprouting through a sidewalk crack pulls it back. Or, it might get pulled back by the sight of dirt and wriggling worms in a place that, just a few weeks prior, was a pile of dried leaves. That soil will nourish plants that will, in turn, nourish me.

I recognize the turmoil, cynicism, and imbalances of our

OUR INHERITED WISDOM

times, yet my rural upbringing instilled in me that reverence is fundamental to life. Microbes mattered, as did insects and seeds, and the community gatherings for worship and helping one another when needed. There was an understanding that no matter how advanced humans become with our inventions, we are part of a living web. Like all mammals, our bodies still need air, food, water, and face-to-face connections between our selves and environments.

The tufts of grass, billowing rain clouds, and splendor of sunsets are persistent in trying to get our attention. Like loving friends, they invite us to slow down, put the phone aside, and notice them. If we are quiet enough, perhaps we'll rest in awareness that they are always with us, supporting us. Perhaps when we stop and commune with Mother Nature long enough, we'll be surprised to find a neglected gem in ourselves—such as, kindness, tolerance, humility and love.

Wise poets, saints, and sages like Halas remind us that enlightenment is found within the everyday. When we can see that the wind does not cling and the sun freely offers light without expectation, we know all that love is. This wisdom becomes more challenging to follow, as our mindscapes become the new commercial frontier. Yet, I choose to claim my own mind territory and fill it with raw wonder until there is only alert stillness. This is a stillness that is impervious to outer distractions but deeply cares for our collective well-being.

EARTH

PRACTICE

This practice supports awareness of your inner light.

Prepare—
- Choose a time and place—indoors or outdoors—with minimal distractions.
- Sit comfortably on an even, firm surface. Rest the backs of your hands on your thighs.
  Release tension around your temples and the corners of your eyes, nose, and mouth.

Practice—
- Imagine yourself as a flowering plant.
  - Relax your hips toward the earth. Lengthen your spine upward as though it were a stem. Like leaves, allow your shoulders to gracefully release away from the neck.
- Breathe with ease for 7-to-10 breaths.
  - On inhale: Imagine your body absorbing the light of the sun.
  - On exhale: Imagine that the sunlight penetrates more and more deeply into your core. Let it spark a feeling of ever-present love.
- Breathe gently and freely for another 7-to-10 breaths.
  - On inhale: Invite the glow from your heart to slowly extend to the inner surface of your body.
  - On exhale: Relax and allow the rays to recede back into your heart center. Release any remaining tension around your chest, abdomen, throat, and back of the skull, as though clearing space for your inner light to shine more brightly.

OUR INHERITED WISDOM

- Sit quietly for several minutes.
  - In this stillness, imagine you are a plant blossoming love and light.
  - Imagine all of life is a garden filled with plants blossoming love and light.

Transition Back into Your Day—
- Place your palms together in front of your heart and gently bow your head.
- Breathe smoothly and evenly for a few breaths. Release the backs of your hands onto your thighs and slowly lift your head.
- Gently return to your day.

EARTH

THE MOUNTAIN

The birds have vanished down the sky.
Now the last cloud drains away.

We sit together, the mountain and me,
until only the mountain remains.

Li Po
Trans. by Sam Hamill

A low cloud hid the mountain peak. There was only a hint of a rise in the land, peeking out under the billowy, grey shape. It seemed as though the mountain had been tucked in by the sky for a much-needed nap from eons of activity. Not only had it been in formation for millions of years, but also it had undergone countless seasonal shifts, bringing bursts of water, wildlife, and color to its slopes.

The shrouded mountain reminded me of stalwart people who are always behind the scenes in life. There are the ones whom I have never met, such as the prophets, saints and spiritual masters, whose wisdom flows like ripples of grace through life. Then, there are people like my ancestors, who are the foundation of my abilities to negotiate life's ups and downs.

I particularly think of my father, Bob Vogt, who had a steady, easeful presence. Much of his work life was spent in

OUR INHERITED WISDOM

silence as he cared for the plants, the soil, and the large farm vehicles used for tilling, sowing and harvesting. He understood the rhythms of nature. As a farmer, his life decisions were intimately linked to the amount and timing of the rains and snows. In a semi-arid region, his patience required a level of faith and confidence in natural abundance and divine will that most of us who live in urban areas cannot even imagine.

If you asked him if he were worried about whether it would rain, he'd answer, "It will rain. It always has." He would say that it doesn't help to worry about the weather, or any of those things, or people, over which you have no control. Instead, he modeled doing the best we can by making consistent and informed effort, and being sincerely grateful for what we have. Even with his discipline and sense of responsibility, he seemed to have an ample inner pool of humor and lightheartedness to keep him and those around him grounded.

A ray of sun broke through the clouds, revealing the upper edges of the mountain. Even though my memory could direct me to where I was going, I felt a tangible relief to see the mountain. The peaceful, undulating ridgeline gave me a solid sense that I was oriented in the right direction—toward the stillness of the mountain.

THE MOUNTAIN

PRACTICE

This practice supports gratitude for help you have received in life.

Prepare—
- Begin seated.
  - Gently shrug your shoulders up and down a few times.
  - Open your mouth wide and yawn, or try to yawn. Smile.
  - Shake through your wrists. Open and squeeze your fingers.

Practice—
- If comfortable, close your eyes. Otherwise, keep your eyes slightly open, with a soft gaze.
- Allow your hands to rest comfortably in your lap.
- Bring to mind someone who has helped you in your life. This might be someone who genuinely wanted the very best for you.
  - Allow yourself to wholeheartedly think of that person. If your mind wavers, gently bring your thoughts back to thinking about that person.
  - Imagine every cell in your body thinking of that person who truly loved and helped you.
  - Take 3-to-4 smooth, even breaths.
  - Then, silently utter "thank you" a few times, from the depths of sincerity.

OUR INHERITED WISDOM

Transition Back into Your Day—
- Sit quietly, for as long as you feel comfortable.
- When you are ready, return to your day.

THE MOUNTAIN

PAUSE

I saw myself when I shut my eyes:
space, space
where I am and am not.

Octavio Paz
Trans. by Muriel Rukeyser

In the northern hemisphere, the spring equinox is near. The migratory birds have begun to return to the local waterways, and the tree buds are transforming into flowers and leaves. As the days grow longer, the sun seems to glow a bit brighter and be burning away the remains of winter.

In the midst of the shifts, I find myself anticipating each sign of spring. I'm caught in the flavor of this time of year, when the gray gives way to new life. My thoughts turn like seasonal changes, with one seamlessly morphing into the other. The equinox offers me an invitation to pause and notice the ever-transforming cycles of life.

Poetry invites the reader to frequently pause. That pause bridges the moving extravaganza of colors, shapes and sounds with the calm unity of all. Within the space between words, phrases, and sentences, there is freedom to be pleasantly suspended between hindsight and anticipation. I allow myself to linger there in momentary silence.

With the pauses, Octavio Paz draws us to the endless center of all. That center externalizes itself into another

OUR INHERITED WISDOM

point—another word or phrase—and creates a relationship between the two. Throughout the center stays steady, allowing the words and movements to brush over its surface. I am reminded that we too have a calm essence, which is said to reside and glow deeply within us.

When I was a child, I loved to sing the phrase, "This little light of mine, let it shine, let it shine." At the time, I had no awareness of how easily life and all its experiences can cover over that little light. Nor did I realize the effort and courage it would take to truly let that inner radiance shine into the world. Yet, Paz and other poets artfully reveal the way to live within the pauses. There, we each can realize the truth of our being.

As life unfolds, I will linger between yesterday and tomorrow, night and day, and the space between the words. On the surface, the swaying of thoughts and activities will still happen, but I'll leave room for the sun to shine between the branches in my mind.

PAUSE

PRACTICE

This practice supports awareness of inner light.

Prepare—
- Sit upright, either on a chair or on a cushion on the floor. Your eyes may be gently closed, or in a soft gaze.
- Stretch out through your arms, hands, and the sides of your torso.

Practice—
- Place your left palm over your spiritual heart-center (this is, symbolically, at the center of your chest). Then, place your right palm over the top of your left hand.
- Three times:
  - Inhale—Reach your hands upward and slightly outward from your heart center (will be like you are reaching toward the sky, with your arms in an open "V" shape). Imagine you are reaching up and gathering the light of the sun into your palms.
    - If you follow a particular faith, imagine that these and the following movements as a prayer.
  - Exhale—Bring your palms back over your heart.
- With your fingertips, lightly touch the following areas of your body and head. Imagine as though you are placing light in those areas.
  - Feet, ankles, knees, hips, lower belly, navel area, upper chest/shoulders by crossing your forearms across your body to take the opposite hand to each shoulder, elbows, wrists, hands (gently stroking each hand with the other), and throat.

OUR INHERITED WISDOM

- ○ Temples, jaw, nose, mouth, eyes, cheekbones, ears, back of your skull, center of forehead, and top of your skull.
- Let your hands return to your heart-center, and let them gently rest there, with minimal tension in the shoulders, arms, or hands.
  - ○ Six-to-twelve breaths, according your comfort and time.
    - Inhale—Imagine as though the light is glowing deep within your heart-center.
    - Exhale—Imagine as though the glow of the light rises up from the core of your heart-center along the spine to the upper, inside center of your skull.
      - Briefly linger at the end of your exhale and imagine the entire inner surface of your skull is glowing.
    - On the next inhale, reach your arms upward and outward with open palms. Imagine you are returning the light to its source. Silently say, "Thank you."

Transition Back into Your Day—
- Release your hands onto your thighs, with the palms upward.
- Simply sit and breathe until you are ready to re-enter your day.

PAUSE

SILENT SONG

Silently a flower blooms,
in silence it falls away;
Yet here now, at this moment, at this place,
> the whole of the flower, the whole of the world is blooming.
This is the talk of the flower, the truth of the blossom;
The glory of eternal life is fully shining here.

Zenkei Shibayama
Trans. by Sumiko Kudo

In a few days, the North Pole will be tilted furthest away from the sun. This phenomenon, called solstice, has a different affect on the earth's hemispheres. It signifies winter in the north and summer in the south.

Even with the increasing number of natural disasters and unseasonal temperatures, the solstice is a reminder of the ongoing cycle of life. Days grow longer on one side of the planet, and shorter on the other. Flowers bloom and fade. The moon waxes and wanes. As I saw in my own family this past year, loved ones die and new ones arrive.

Solstice also reminds us to pause, to be still. The word solstice stems from two Latin words *sol* and *sistere*, translated as "sun" and "to stand still." This is because the angle of the earth's axis in relationship to the sun stops at either the

OUR INHERITED WISDOM

northern or southernmost limit before it reverses directions. There is stillness in the swaying.

Throughout the world, prophets and sage masters amplify our earthly message. Our earth's lullaby quietly rocks us from side to side. It invites us to know that her silent song is our song. Silence is at the heart of all. We are encouraged to rejoice in stillness, and to be rejoiced.

Cues to eternal joy are everywhere, and I find a certain humor in that. We are always searching, or inventing, new ways to find what is already there. A flower, as in Zenkei Shibayama's poem, speaks the silent life of all things. In our breath there is a pause as the air moves in and out.

Silence invigorates life and is the fountainhead of peace. This inspires me to pause and smile. Then, repeat, again and again until only silence remains.

SILENT SONG

PRACTICE

This practice helps bring awareness that all directions radiate from the heart.

Prepare—
- Place your phone and other digital tools in airplane mode.
  - Remove watches and activity trackers from your wrist. Remove your shoes.
- This is a standing practice. Have a chair nearby.
- Shake out your right side, first your right arm and then your right leg. Repeat, on the left side. Shake each limb for about a minute.
- Playfully dance around for a few moments.

Practice—
- Staying in one place, slowly turn in a circle, counterclockwise.
- Staying in one place, slowly make quarter-turns to your right.
  - Pause at each quarter-turn.
  - Elbows bent, palms upward and to the sides, as though holding flowers in the palms of your hands.
    - Note: if you cannot visualize quarter-turns, try imagining turning to the four horizontal directions. Or, imagine that you are standing in the center of an analog clock. You begin facing the number 12, and then, turn and pause at the numbers 3, 6, 9, and 12.

OUR INHERITED WISDOM

- Standing, reach your fingers toward the earth. Then, overhead.
- Bring your palms together in front of your heart. Take three breaths. Imagine that all directions meet at the core of your heart. Smile.

Transition Back into Your Day –
- Come to a comfortable seated position.
- Pause and sit quietly for a few minutes before returning to your day.

SILENT SONG

SOLITUDE

Which is worth more, a crowd of thousands,
or your own genuine solitude?
Freedom, or power over an entire nation?

A little while alone in your room
will prove more valuable than anything else
that could ever be given you.

Rumi
Trans. by Coleman Barks

The back screen door swung closed behind me. I paused for a moment to ponder my options for this warm fall morning. I could visit our farm horse Shorty out in the pasture, or climb up the ladder on the windmill, romp with the dog, or maybe check on the dirt hole that my older sister and I had excavated the day before. A cloud that looked like a dragon caught my eye. It was turning into a flock of sheep. I plopped down on my back and I was soon at play with the daytime sky.

Such solitude was normal for me. The adults around me were from generations of farmers who modeled comfort with being alone—as much as being together with others. From an early age, I was in training to have ease with both being by myself and relating to the community and surrounding nature. Whether doing simple chores such as feeding the outdoor cats

OUR INHERITED WISDOM

—we always had a dozen or so—or being free to explore, I was encouraged to be responsibly independent, yet acutely aware that I am part of the greater society and rhythms of life.

It has been decades since I've lived on our family wheat farm in Western Kansas, but my inner landscape reflects my childhood experience. Unlike the current references to the "flattening" of psyche, the nearly uninterrupted horizon at my home bred a sense of expansive possibilities within me. It shaped a sense of inner peace and a capacity for selfhood where I am comfortable with being with myself, being cyber-free for a while, and having an unscheduled calendar for a period of time. I've yet to find solace with being in the deep wilderness alone in a tent, but have roamed around the globe, trusting the inner way—these are my findings garnered in the flatlands.

The world's ancient poets and saints, like the 13th century poet Rumi, lauded the jewels of genuine solitude—inner contentment, steadfastness, clarity, light-heartedness, creativity, and compassion. When each person is rooted inwardly, a thriving community can arise, much like a forest of hundreds of individual trees. Concepts such as "one and many" lose their meaning because all are part of the whole, and the whole is made up of the parts.

Often solitude is equated with the modern form of loneliness and isolation that makes us fearful, clouds our minds, weakens our immunity to the commercial din, and leaves us susceptible to letting others shape our thoughts and lives. Yet, the modern version is almost the opposite of the solitude that humans have known from the earliest times,

SOLITUDE

where the well-being of both the human and earthly forests begins with the strength of each sapling. This inspires me to make space for solitude in my life, e.g., by being cyber-free for one day each week.

PRACTICE

This short practice is a reminder that we constantly interact with the world through our senses, breath, hands, and feet.

Prepare—
- Sit with your spine upright.
  - If you are in a chair, rest the soles of your feet on the floor.
- Scrunch up your face a few times. Open and close your jaw. Stretch out your hands.
- Vigorously rub your palms together until you feel some warmth in your hands.
- Be aware of your senses:
  - Eyes: With your eyes closed lightly, touch your eyelids, feeling the warmth. Allow your eyes to relax.
  - Lips: Move your fingertips to your lips and let them rest there, allowing the corners of your mouth to relax. Soften your chin and release any unnecessary tension in your face.
  - Ears: Place your hands over your ears and take a few breaths.
- Release your palms into your lap.

OUR INHERITED WISDOM

Practice—
- Bring your hands in front of your face with your palms facing you, and your fingers pointing toward one another.
- With your fingers, seal off the sensory inputs:
  - Index fingers gently resting on your eyelids;
  - Middle fingers resting lightly on the fleshy part of your nose;
  - Ring fingers resting above the lips on the outer corners of your mouth;
  - Little fingers resting below the lips on the outer corners of your mouth;
  - Thumbs resting on your ear lobes.
- Breath 6-12 smooth, even inhales and exhales (with the fingers lightly sealing off the eyes, nose, mouth, and ears).
- Let your hands rest in your lap.
  - Your eyes could be closed or have a soft gaze.

Transition Back into Your Day—
- Sit for a few moments before returning to your day.

SOLITUDE

STILLNESS

Clear full moon,
The night is very still.
My heart sounds
Like a bell.

Japanese Folk Song
Trans. by Kenneth Rexroth

I awoke to a silent, clear morning after a full moon. The prior three days had been filled with high winds and heavy rainfall, and the forecast was for continued thundershowers and flooding. So the quiet was a welcomed pause between storms. Only a distant church bell stirred the peacefulness.

The bell rang seven times—a call to the morning mass, for my neighbors and for me to sit in stillness. The bell falls silent and my neighbor and I commune with the divine presence, each in our own way. Outside, the winter sun begins to rise in silence and the light of the full moon fades. For now, all is unruffled by the winds of the mind.

Before long, the storms will begin even more forcefully, toppling long-standing trees and dislodging birds' nests and routines. Yet, I know the bell will still ring and that, beneath the din, stillness awaits. It is this knowingness that causes me to rise morning after morning and be still. How else will I find the well-being and courage to breathe freely and trust that the storm will subside?

OUR INHERITED WISDOM

As I read this folk song, I reflect on the ancient view of moonlight as the revealer of the mystery and fear within our souls. The moon was considered the measurer of time, with its five phases, and the mover of water—rains and tides—and the seasons. The Indo-European root of the word moon—"me"—connotes measure. The full moon day is an auspicious time to pause in the midst of the turbulence of life.

Similarly, bells have ancient significance. They are a call to awaken and to be still, whether in prayer, meditation, or as protection from an approaching enemy. For some, the sound resulting silence of a bell is considered to have supernatural properties and can be heard far beyond the limits of time. A carefully crafted bell produces a clean, clear tone and symbolizes eternal peace. The ringing of a bell can chase away less desirable emotions, such as fear, and make way for a still, inner home for lasting joy, love, and peace.

A full moon and the chime of bells are examples of ordinary experiences that remind us to pause and savor quietude. Pausing in silence nourishes the soul and is beneficial for our physical and emotional health. It gives us a regular break from our media addictions, which stress our nervous systems and can exhaust us emotionally. Consistent pausing in silence eases our cortisol levels, and supports overall well-being. Regular pauses deepen our human capacity to sustain steady, inner stillness unruffled by the ups and downs of life.

STILLNESS

PRACTICE

This practice invites you to slow down and sit in silence for a few moments whenever you can.

Prepare—
- Remove any potential distractions—for example, take off your watch, and put your phone on airplane mode.
- If you have a small bell, ring it once before beginning.
- Seated: Spine upright, shoulders relaxed, and if you are in a chair, both feet on the floor.

Practice—
- Silence your senses:
    - Eyes—Close your eyes. Lightly rest the pads of your index fingers on your eyelids. Let your ring, middle, and little finger pads rest on your cheeks.
    - Ears—Close off sounds by lightly pressing your thumbs on your front ear flaps.
- Breathe seven (7) even, smooth breaths, with your eyes and ears closed.

Transition Back into Your Day—
- Release your hands into your lap. Your eyes may be closed or in a soft gaze.
- Sit quietly for 3 minutes or longer.
- When you are ready, return to your day.

Divine Freedom
LOVE

MIST

>   What
>   Is the
>   Root of all these
>   Words?
>
>   One thing: love.
> But a love so deep and sweet
> It needed to express itself
> With scents, sounds, colors
>   That never before
>   Existed.
>
>   Hafiz
> *Trans. by Daniel Landinsky*

The morning sky has been grey and misty this past week. People scurry along the sidewalks with their chins tucked into the fronts of their jackets. In the coffee shop, the conversations are about the gloomy weather, with wishes that it would get a little brighter.

    Instead of feeling dreary, I feel joyful within the grey. It is as though the earth has merged into the vast sky. Or, that the sky has come to visit the earth, to show us that it is always there, holding and flowing through us. The greyness softens edges and boundaries. It gives everything a quality of being infinite.

OUR INHERITED WISDOM

When the grey gives way to a clearer sky, the world begins to sparkle in its different colors and shapes. Birds sing, and the steps of people on the street seem to lighten. Surprisingly, some even pause and look up at the sky in a way that appears they are seeing it for the first time.

The grey invites us to realize anew the beauty of the world. Being enveloped in grey along with our surroundings can feel like a tender caress. It can stir a sense of a sweet, loving Presence that is more immense than any other love we have known. This love is love itself: luminous; omniscient (all-knowing); virtuous; and everlasting (l.o.v.e.).

Prophets, sages and great poets like Hafiz remind us that our world is an expression of a love that never ends. As an integral part of the world, we too, in our heart of hearts, are love. We forget this and go looking for the love that we already are. There is still our pain and discomfort, but beneath it all is the love that sustains.

Sacred poetry and misty mornings are outer reminders that we are living expressions of love. A complete shift into this knowingness takes long-term, continuous practice of daily meditation and/or prayer. Yet, little things also help. This inspires me to feel a little lighter and more hopeful every time I say, hear, write, or see the word "love."

MIST

PRACTICE

This practice supports awareness of love from the inside out.

Prepare—
- Hug yourself. Shift so that your other arm is on top, and re-hug yourself.
- Gently squeeze each arm, one arm at a time, using the opposite hand. Begin at your shoulder, then move down to your elbow and then your wrist and hand.
- Pretend to wash your face with your fingertips.
    - For example, gently brush your fingertips up from the eyebrows to the hairline, and then down across the temples and cheeks.

Practice—
- Find a comfortable seated position, either on a chair or on the floor.
    - Allow your spine to be in a neutral, upright position and your breath to be free and unhindered.
- Rest the back of one hand, i.e., palm upward, in the center of your lap.
- Then, as though holding hands with yourself, rest the other palm in the palm in your lap (i.e., the palm is upward on your lower palm; and downward on the upper. The palms are at a 90-degree angle).
    - Imagine that your lower palm is the hand of your most loving friend.
        - Relax the muscles in that arm. Let that relaxation stem from your heart-center, shoulder blades, shoulder, entire arm, and fingers.

OUR INHERITED WISDOM

- ○ Let the other hand relax and receive the loving support.
- Allow your eyes to gently close, or find a soft gaze. Relax the muscles across your face. Allow your breath to be soft and smooth.
- Stay for as long as comfortable, preferably at least three minutes on each side.

Transition Back into Your Day—
- Place the backs of both hands on your thighs. Invite a few full, gentle inhalations and exhalations. Allow for a slight pause between your inhales and exhales.
- Sit quietly for a few moments.
- Give yourself a hug and sincerely say to yourself, "I love you."
- When you are ready, transition back into your day.

MIST

THE QUILT

And
yet one word
frees us from all the weight and pain in life:

That word is
love.

Sophocles
Trans. by Robert Fitzgerald

I noticed a small rip in the flowery blue fabric. This caused me to look a little more closely at the quilt that I had had for about three decades. It seemed impossible that wear would ever show on something that had been carefully stitched by one of my grandmothers—my mother's mother. She was a corseted, strong woman who had always seemed to be the essence of durability. Her patterns were as firm as the shapes on the quilt.

More than one hundred clusters of colorful hexagons span the quilt's surface. Like many who have little money, my grandmother let nothing go to waste. She had pieced together a home by patiently and creatively using and re-using whatever was available. The quilt, which is aptly called "Grandmother's Flower Garden," represents how she turned scraps into a lasting story of quiet love.

OUR INHERITED WISDOM

The hexagonal form of the quilt pieces is the most efficient use of material. Bees construct their honeycombs with hexagonal shapes, where each side fits together without leaving gaps. Hexagons are found elsewhere in nature, such as in DNA, snowflakes, and crystals, as well as a large cloud formation over the north pole of the planet Saturn. The heart of two interlocking triangles—one facing upward and one downward — forms a hexagon, symbolically representing eternal, divine love flowing between heaven and earth.

True love seldom, if ever, looks for recognition. It just continues to express itself in different ways throughout our lives. For the most part, it is masked over by the despair and stress of mortal existences. Yet, there are the bees diligently pollinating plants and making honeycombs, and the quilting bees of women sitting around a table, stitching together the front and back of quilts. Their efforts and work remain mostly anonymous until there is a tear, or a decline in their population. Then we notice that the loving infrastructure is more fragile that we had imagined.

For a long while, I had dismissed Sophocles' words on love. They seemed to offer easy terminology to respond to the suffering of others. The simple phrase "frees us" shifted my perspective inward to recognize that, at the core of kindness, compassion, and service is a hexagonal garden of love. To know—and to be—that love is a lifetime of focus and work. I hope to take one small step each day by noticing a bit more of the lessons within everyday life.

THE QUILT

PRACTICE

This practice supports your awareness of love.

Prepare—
- Turn your phone and other devices off or to airplane mode.
- Find a comfortable seated position, either in a chair or on the floor.
  - Sit with enough support under you so that your spine can easily lengthen.
  - If needed, stretch out through your arms, upward, outward, forward, and slightly back.
  - Allow your hands to relax in your lap.
  - Soften your gaze.
- Take a few smooth, easy breaths, perhaps noticing the gentle opening and releasing in your chest.

Practice—
- Imagine yourself surrounded by six luminous orbs, each infused with love.
  - One sphere beneath you, one above you, one around each shoulder, and one around each hip. (This is like a circle of love around you.)
    - With each inhale;
      - Invite each orb to slowly grow outward until it slightly overlaps with the adjoining sphere.
    - With each exhale;
      - Allow the glow of each orb to be a little brighter and softer.

OUR INHERITED WISDOM

- Rest one hand on top of the other over the center of your chest, symbolically, your heart-center. Imagine that beneath your hands, there is another glowing ball of love.
  - With each inhale, invite the love from the core of your heart to grow outward until it enfolds all the other circles.
  - With each exhale, allow yourself to be bathed in love. Every cell, every atom of your being is soaked in love. For just one moment, allow yourself to let go into this ocean of love. Be love.
- Allow your hands to relax back into your lap. Breathe in. Breathe out.

Transition Back into Your Day—
- Sit quietly for a few moments.
- Lightly touch your nose, mouth, eyes, ears, cheeks, and skull. As you do this, invite the memory of ever-present love to settle into all your senses and your mind.
- When you are ready, return to your day.

THE QUILT

TIMELESS LOVE

My bounty is as boundless as the sea,
My love as deep; the more I give to thee,
The more I have, for both are infinite.

William Shakespeare

It is stormy outside. The winds are unpredictable, and the rainwaters are filling the rivers and creeks. There are regular alerts to possible flooding and landslides. Trees have fallen, and no doubt there will be lasting shifts in the landscape.

The intensity of the weather reminds me of the sages' wisdom that life is ever-changing. One moment, we feel as though everything is stable and predictable. And the next moment, we are in unfamiliar territory. Big life events, storms, and major shifts in the outer world have a way of revealing the tenderness and fragility of existence.

Saints and sages tell us that these cracks in our routines offer a chance to greet our inner self, the one who has been there all along and will always be. At the heart of hearts, nothing changes. There is only pure, boundless love. It is the love that holds us and gives us the clarity, creativity, and capacity to serve the world with loving knowingness, equanimity, and compassion.

I feel that Shakespeare gives voice to timeless love through the famed words of Juliet. These lines stand alone, like Juliet on her balcony as she speaks them into the darkness. It is almost as though Shakespeare is reminding us to unearth our deepest passions and to know that there is only one desire that can free us—and that is to know that we are love. The death of the two lovers to me is a symbolic end to longing and expectation. It occurs when the separate rivers of life have returned to the infinite sea of love.

Centuries later, these lines continue to inspire us. Regardless of whether they are for romantic love or for our highest calling of love, they bring us together in the name of love. This inspires me to begin each day with thanks for another day of loving.

TIMELESS LOVE

PRACTICE

This practice supports awareness of the loving support in the world around us.

Prepare—
- Set your phone on airplane mode.
- Interlace your fingers, stretch your fingers out in front of you, and reverse your palms. Invite two to three full breaths into your lungs.
- Let your hands relax into your lap and notice their natural weight on your thighs.

Practice—
- With your hands resting in your lap, recall being in a place, or situation, where you felt completely safe, trusting, supported, calm, joyful, and maybe even in the presence of unimaginable magnificence.
    - If you have difficulty doing this, slowly look around at your surroundings and find something from the natural world that you find beautiful—a flower, a plant, a wooden floor, a cotton fabric. (Ideally, the choice is not an image of another human.)
- Invite this memory (of being totally safe, trusting, supported, in awe, and/or being loved) to seep into your awareness. Imagine this sweet memory is spreading throughout your entire being.
    - You may wish to imagine that with each inhale, this sense is slowly expanding outward from deep within your heart center. Like rays of the sun, it radiates out in all directions. And, with each exhale, you can savor

OUR INHERITED WISDOM

- the sweetness as it nourishes each cell of your body.
  - Take your time with this.
    - You may feel or notice resistance. If you do, try to gently coax your awareness toward this subtler, more peaceful memory.
  - Once you feel the sweetness having gently filled your entire being, sit quietly.
- Imagine: awakening into this feeling; moving through your day; eating your meals; talking and interacting with others; and then, falling asleep, still with this feeling.
  - Know that this sweet, gentle part of you is always there.
- Throughout the practice, invite the facial, neck and shoulder muscles to release tension. Invite a soft gaze into your eyes. Your breath is easy and relaxed.

Transition Back into Your Day—
- Invite this feeling to settle into the tips of each of your fingers.
- Take your time before returning to your day. Instead, consider sealing in this practice within the environment around you through touching your surroundings.
(If you are in a public place, you can imagine touching your surroundings.)
- When you are ready, return to your day.

TIMELESS LOVE

LOVING NATURE

Look
what happens to the scale
when love
holds
it.

It
stops
working.

Kabir
Trans. by Daniel Ladinsky

Looking out the plane's window, I was mesmerized by the curvy pathways of the waters and the undulating contours of the earth. Every bend in a river and every rise in the land seemed like individual brushstrokes shaping an unending scene of existence itself.

There was something peaceful about having a bird's-eye view of our planet earth. Within the landscape below, nearly nine million species were coming and going. Flowers were blooming, butterflies were coming out, and petals and wings were falling. Viewed from above, it looked whole and serenely beautiful, free of all harm.

This flight experience reminded me that the mind is like the sky. When it is cloud-free, the view and perspective are

OUR INHERITED WISDOM

clear. But, most days there are clouds covering all or part of the sky. The cloudier it is, the less clear the view, and the more likely we are to focus on the play of the clouds and forget the expansive, serene clarity that is always there.

It takes effort not to cloud the mind or feed its tendency to self-absorption. With a constant stream of impressions coming in from commercial entities and our social communities, our minds have come to long for continual stimulation. When we try to interrupt the techno-cravings, we look for a predictable engagement of time and environment, e.g., by choosing an online tool for meditation, mindfulness or yoga.

When I step back and truly *look*, as the 5th century poet Kabir suggests, I realize life is not a commodity to be earned or bartered. Instead, it is held in the eternal embrace of love. Like the sky holding the cloud, love doesn't grasp or cling to us. It just patiently holds all of life. And, as with Kabir's imagery of the scale, love doesn't erase the world. Instead, it is the doorway within the world to infinite peace and calmness.

Sages and other wise beings, such as Kabir, speak of our essence as limitless love. When the mind is clear, it is luminous and filled with boundless truth, light, and joy.

LOVING NATURE

PRACTICE
This practice supports awareness of peace and serenity.

Prepare—
- Turn all electronic devices to airplane mode.
    - If you are wearing a watch and/or any other wrist items, remove it/them. Ideally, place these items in another room.
- Seated, allow your hands to relax, with the backs of your hands resting on your thighs. Relax the center of your palms and the fingers.
    - If you are seated in a chair, rest both of your feet on the floor.
- Eyes closed, or open with a soft gaze, gently bring your attention to the movement of the breath. Without strain, slowly exhale. Slowly inhale.
- Release any unneeded tension along your temples, forehead, and the rest of your face.

Practice—
- Lift the hands away from the thighs.
    - Bend the elbows so that the forearms are somewhat parallel to the floor.
    - Turn your palms downward and let your hands relax. (Fingers dangling downward.)
- Rotate the forearms so that your hands slowly rotate inward toward one another, then upward, and then outward.
    - Keep a relaxed feeling in your hands.
        - Elbows are softly bent and palms relaxed and upward.

OUR INHERITED WISDOM

- With your eyes open or closed, pause for a minute or so. Soft, gentle breaths.
- Repeat above for three or more times.
  - Invite a feeling of simultaneously letting go and receptivity during the gesture and then pause.
  - If it feels comfortable, repeat silently, "I welcome eternal truth, light, and love" during the pause.

Transition Back into Your Day—
- Relax the backs of your hands onto your thighs. Allow the mind to follow the inhales and exhales for four to five minutes.
- Then, transition back into your day.

LOVING NATURE

LOVE

All you need is love, love
Love is all you need.

John Lennon and Paul McCartney

The mirror snapped off the passenger side of my car. It took me a second to realize that I had been in the blind spot of the parked car and as I had passed, the driver had opened his door. Fortunately, he and his car were fine, and the mirror was the only damage.

When I dropped the car at the body shop to have the mirror fixed, the mechanic was playing some music from the Beatles. I didn't think too much about it until the next day, when my mind kept repeating "Love. Love is all you need." It has been two weeks, and it seems that these lyrics have moved in for a while, with thoughts of love seeping in at unexpected times during the day.

Love seems to be everywhere. By being more in tune with love, I realize that we hear, see, say, and read the word love countless times in a day. Apparently it is one of the 400 most frequently used words in English. We study love, and are entertained by love, and live love. Mythologies across the globe honor love. It has shaped some of the timeless operas and literature, such as *Romeo and Juliet*.

Love sells phones, shoes, fast food, skin products, eyeglasses and cars. It shows up in idioms and is venerated by world religions.

OUR INHERITED WISDOM

Older languages have more than one word for love: Hebrew, two; Greek, three; Persian, 30; and, Sanskrit, 96. Yet, in English, we only have one. I choose to see the singular word not as a dearth in our language but as an invitation to reflect on the purest love—the Love that is the thread connecting all loves. This love can be considered synonymous with consciousness, or the divine. A love that loves without reason.

I'm appreciating that my mirror was shattered. It gave me a chance to have my inner mirror focus on love. Now, I am wondering if I owe the mechanic an extra fee for the mind tune-up.

In the meantime, my intention is to be more aware of the ways my life is supported by love. My hope is that through that awareness, tendencies of pity and judgment will soften into compassion and equanimity. And, from there, I will see if fresh actions and habits arise that are more reflective of love.

LOVE

PRACTICE

This practice is more like a prayer of appreciation for the all-pervasive support of love in life.

Prepare—
- Sit upright on a chair or the floor.
- Notice and release any tension around your legs, hip creases, belly, chest, throat and face.
- This practice involves placing one hand on different parts of the body, and then quietly acknowledging ways love touches our worldly life. You may wish to read through this a few times and then personalize it.

Practice—
- Place one hand on *your lowest belly.*
  - Silently say, "I acknowledge the soil, its capacity to hold and nourish me, and all those who protect and care for the soil. I acknowledge the plants, insects, birds, and animals, their strength and vulnerability, and those who protect and care for them. And, I acknowledge my digestive system and its ability to process food to nourish my body. I appreciate my feet and legs and my ability to stand and to make choices to do the least harm possible." Take a few breaths.
- Place one hand *below your navel.*
  - Silently say, "I acknowledge water, its capacity to sustain and cleanse me, and all those who protect and care for the waters. I also acknowledge my renal system and its role in nourishing and cleansing my body. I appreciate my ability to move and to create." Take a few breaths.

OUR INHERITED WISDOM

- Place one hand on *your navel*.
  - Silently say, "I acknowledge the sun, its capacity to nourish and warm me and the world around me, and the light it provides for me to see. I also acknowledge my emotions and the ability to feel and experience the world." Take a few breaths.
- Place one hand on *your throat*.
  - Silently say, "I acknowledge the air and wind, their capacity to nourish me through sound and breath, and all those who protect and care for them. I also acknowledge my throat and its capacity to carry the breath, food, my voice, and the messages in the nervous system to and from the brain. I appreciate my brain and senses for the capacity they give me to interact in the world." Take a few breaths.
- Place one hand on the *center of your chest, the symbolic heart center*.
  - Silently say, "I acknowledge ever-present love and its sister qualities of compassion, peace, joy, kindness. I appreciate the capacity to feel, and act with, true compassion for those who are suffering from war, violence, abuse, hunger, dislocation, injury, and illness. I acknowledge the teachers, poets, and writers who inspire true love and the grace of peace and freedom." Take a few breaths.
- Place one hand on the *top of your head*.
  - Silently say, "I acknowledge the ocean of love." Take a few breaths.

LOVE

Transition Back into Your Day—
- Sit quietly for a few moments, with the eyes and ears tuned inward.
- Place your hands over your heart and pause for a moment.
- When you are ready, return to your day.

OUR INHERITED WISDOM

SOURCES, CREDITS, AND PERMISSION ACKNOWLEDGMENTS

Every effort has been made to trace the copyright holders of poetry in this book. The author apologizes if any poetry or other material has been included without permission. If I/we have missed any attributions, please contact the author and the necessary corrections will be made in a future edition. Gratitude is due to the following for permission to include poems or extracts from poetry in copyright.

"All You Need Is Love," words and music by John Lennon and Paul McCartney, copyright © 1967 Sony/ATV Music Publishing LLC. Copyright renewed. All rights administered by Sony/ATV Music Publishing LLC, 424 Church Street, Suite 1200, Nashville, TN 37219. International Copyright Secured All Rights Reserved. Reprinted by permission of Hal Leonard Corporation.

"Are you jealous of the ocean's generosity?," "If you want money more," "Which is worth more, a crowd of thousands," and "Spring overall" by Rumi, translated by Coleman Barks, from the MAYPOP publication *Birdsong*. Copyright © 1993 by Coleman Barks and used with his permission.

"There's a tree that existed before the woods" by Han Shan, translated by Tony Barnstone and Chou Ping; from THE ANCHOR BOOK OF CHINESE POETRY: FROM ANCIENT TO CONTEMPORARY, THE FULL 3000-YEAR TRADITION edited by Tony Barnstone and Chou Ping, copyright © 2005 by Tony Barnstone and Chou Ping. Used by permission of Anchor Books, an imprint of the Knopf Doubleday Publishing Group, a division of Penguin Random House LLC. All rights reserved.

"Clear full moon" (XCIX) by Anonymous, and "Not Speaking of the Way" by Yosano Akiko, translated by Kenneth

SOURCES, CREDITS AND PERMISSION, ACKNOWLEDGMENTS

Rexroth, from *One Hundred More Poems from the Japanese.* Copyright © 1977 by Kenneth Rexroth. Reprinted by permission of New Directions Publishing Corp.

"Even If I Repeated Love's Name" by Izumi Shikibu, from *The Ink Dark Moon: Love Poems by Ono No Komachi and Izumi Shi- kibu, Women of the Ancient Court of Japan,* translated by Jane Hirshfield, translation copyright © 1990 by Jane Hirshfield. Used by permission of Vintage Books, an imprint of Knopf Doubleday Publishing Group, a division of Penguin Random House LLC. All rights reserved.

"True love gives us beauty" excerpt by Thich Nhat Hanh. Reprinted from *How to Love* (2015) by Thich Nhat Hanh with permission of Parallax Press, parallax.org.

"To see the world," "God, whose love and joy," excerpt from "I ask all blessings," "The great sea has set me in motion," and "One instant in eternity," from *The Enlightened Heart.* Copyright © 1989 Stephen Mitchell. Reprinted by permission of HarperCollins Publishers.

"What is it you want to change?," "I know a cure for sadness," "I could not lie anymore," "Dear God, please reveal to us," "God has never," "Look what happens to the scale," "Know the true nature of your Beloved," "Tenderly," "I was sad one day," "God dissolved my mind," and "Our hands imbibe like roots," from the Penguin publication *Love Poems from God: Twelve Sacred Voices from the East and West.* Copyright © 2002 by Daniel Ladinsky and used with his permission.

"My bounty is as boundless" from *Romeo and Juliet* (The Pelican Shakespeare) by William Shakespeare, edited by A. R. Braunmuller and Stephen Orgel. Copyright © 2000 by Penguin Random House LLC. Used by permission of Penguin Classics, an imprint of Penguin Publishing Group, a division of Penguin Random House LLC.

OUR INHERITED WISDOM

"A Flower Does Not Talk" by Abbot Zenkei Shibayama from *A Flower Does Not Talk: Zen Essays*. Copyright © 1970 Tuttle Publishing. Reproduced with permission of the publisher.

"Night is passing" by Hakim Omar Khayyám, from *Ecstasy: The World of Sufi Poetry and Prayer*. Copyright © 2007 by Nahid Angha, PhD. Excerpt reproduced with permission of Nahid Angha, PhD.

"My Joy" by Råbi'a, from *Doorkeeper of the Heart: Versions of Rabi'a* by Ra- bi'a al-Adawiyya. Copyright © 2003 Pir Press, Inc. Reproduced with permission of the publisher.

"Pleasant Songs: Part II" edited by Anonymous, translated by Noel Stock, from *Love Poems of Ancient Egypt*. Copyright © 1960 by Ezra Pound, copyright © 1962 by Noel Stock. Reprinted by permission of New Directions Publishing Corp.

"Out beyond ideas," "Keep walking," and "All day and night, music" from *Unseen Rain: Quatrains of Rumi* by Rumi. Copyright © 1986 by John Moyne and Coleman Barks. Reprinted by permission of Coleman Barks.

"Observe your life, between two breaths" by Avicenna, from *Love's Alchemy*. Copyright © 2006 David and Sabrineh Fideler. Reprinted by permission of New World Library.

"Prayer" from *The Past* by Galway Kinnell. Copyright © 1985 by Galway Kinnell. Reprinted by permission of Houghton Mifflin Harcourt Publishing Company. All rights reserved.

"The word comes" excerpt from *Concerning the Book That Is the Body of the Beloved* by Gregory Orr. Copyright © 2005 by Gregory Orr. Reprinted with the permission of The Permissions Company, Inc., on behalf of Copper Canyon Press, www.coppercanyonpress.org.

"God blooms from the shoulder," "How do I listen to others?," "Like a great starving beast," "Complaint," and "What Is the Root?" by Hafiz, from the Penguin publication *The Gift: Poems by Hafiz*. Copyright © 1999 by Daniel Ladinsky and used with his permission.

SOURCES, CREDITS AND PERMISSION, ACKNOWLEDGMENTS

"Utterance" from *The Rain in the Trees* by W. S. Merwin. Copyright © 1988 by W. S. Merwin, used by permission of The Wylie Agency LLC.

"Self inside self" by Lalla, from the MAYPOP publication *Naked Song: Lalla*. Copyright © 1992 by Coleman Barks and used with his permission.

"Vision" from *Selected Poems of Octavio Paz*, p. 65, translated by Muriel Rukeyser. Copyright © 1963 Indiana University Press. Reprinted with permission of Indiana University Press.

"Zazen on Ching-t'ing Mountain" by Li Po, from *Crossing the Yellow River: Three Hundred Poems from the Chinese*, translated by Sam Hamill. Copyright © 2000 by Sam Hamill. Reprinted with permission of The Permission Company, Inc., on behalf of Tiger Bark Press, www.tigerbarkpress.com.

About the Photos
Abigail, Sunny Yellow Daisy. Ian Tuck, Squirrel. InBetweentheBlinks, Smiling Dog. James Wainscoat, Hummingbird. Janis Smits, People in Park. Jennifer Vogt-Crockett, White Daisy and Sunflower. Kate Vogt, Bell, Canyon Light, Clouds, Daffodil, Elm Tree, Ganges River, Garden, Hibiscus, Horses, Kansas Sunrise, Lotus, Meadow,Mountain, Mountain Flower, Pine Tree, Quilt, Reeds, Rhododendron, Roots, Spiral, Spring Blossoms, Stream, Sunset on Ocean, Tulip Tree, and Waterfall. Ims-Ims, Springtime. Rene Bernal, Hillside Play. Victor Larracuente, Rabbit. Chris Barbalis, Field. Holly Deckert, Corn Cobs. Gino Santa Maria, Geese. Brendan Delzin, Turtle. Guzmán Barquín, Moonlight. Dave Herring, Sunrise. Elizabeth Lies, Ocean Sky. Caroline Grondin, Raindrops. Josuha Hoehne, Moonlight. Dew Drops. Matt Gibson, Foggy Forest. Matthew Schwartz, Deer. Nikolai Tsvetkov, German Sheepdog. Osiam, Moon with Sunlight. Steve Byland, Western Coyote.

OUR INHERITED WISDOM

ACKNOWLEDGMENTS

Numerous people have contributed directly or indirectly to this book. I particularly wish to acknowledge the teachers and profes-sionals who helped inspired this book and offer guidance throughout the process. In particular, I would like to thank Phil Cousineau for mentoring, Linda Jay for editing, and Jim Shubin for design. I continue to feel deep joy and gratitude to Jay Rosner for his loving support. There are no words to adequately express my gratitude to Mother Earth and the limitless, loving effulgence of the Divine.

POET INDEX

Akiko, Yosano (Shō Hō) (1878-1942, Japan), 63
'Attār (Attar of Nishapur) (c. 1110–1221, Persia), 57
Avicenna (Abū Alī Sīnā, Ibn Sīnā) (980-1037, Persia), 241
The Bible, 15, 151
Blake, William (1757-1827, England), 1, 271
Egyptian (Unknown), 145
Gibran, Khalil (1883-1931, Mt Lebanon), 51
Hafiz (Hafez) (1320-1389, Persia), 45, 159, 177, 191, 235, 315
Halas, František (1901-1949, Czechoslovakia), 279
Hanh, Thich Nhat (1926-, Vietnam), 75
Hanshan (Hánshān) (9th century, Japan), 39
Hwang Chin-i (1506-1544, Korea), 101
Japanese Folk Song, 309
Kabir (Kabir Das) (c. 1440-1518, India), 333
Khayyám, Hakim Omar (1048-1131, Persia), 247
Kinnell, Galway (1927-2014, United States), 69
Lalla (Lal Diddi, Laleswari, Lal Ded) (c. 14h century, Kashmir), 107
Lennon, John Winston Ono (1940-1980, England), 339
Li Po (Li Bai) (c. 701-762, China), 285
McCartney, Sir James Paul (1940, England), 339
Merwin, W. S. (1927-2019, United States), 21
Mirabai (Mira) (c. 1498-1565, India), 139
Navajo (19th-20th century, Navajo Nation), 215
Orr, Gregory (1927- , United States), 165
Paz, Octavio (1914-1998, Mexico), 291
Rābi'a (717-801, Persia), 227
Rumi (Jala Jalāludin Muhammad Rumi) (1207-1273, Persia), 27, 81, 95, 133, 221, 265, 303
Shakespeare, William (1564-1616, England), 327
Shibayama, Zenkei (1894-1974, Japan), 297
Shikibu, Izumi (c. 974-1034, Japan), 259

OUR INHERITED WISDOM

Silesius, Angelus (Johannes Scheffler) (1624-1677, Bohemia), 33
Sophocles (c. 496-c 405 BCE, Greece), 321
St. Catherine of Siena (1347-1380, Italy), 113
St. Francis of Assisi (1182-1226, Italy), 9, 171
St. John of the Cross (1542-1591, Spain), 197, 203
St. Teresa of Avila (1515-1582), Spain), 119
Sun Bu-er (Sun Pu-erb) (1124-c. 1182, China), 253
Swahili (Unknown), 127
Tukaram (1608-1649, India), 183, 209
Uvavnuk (19th-20th century, Inuit Nation), 87

REFLECTIONS AND PRACTICES INDEX

I. Our True Nature
Connectedness
    Beginning and End, 15, 247
    Inner and Outer Beauty, 9, 39, 51, 75, 127, 139, 159, 191, 215, 265
    Divine in All, 4, 95, 107, 177, 183, 221, 265
    Whole in All, 33, 227
Eternal, Unchanging Self
    Divine, 4, 95, 107, 177, 183, 221, 265
    Eternal, 4, 21, 27, 39, 165, 197, 271
    Heart, 4, 51, 113, 259, 315
    Joy, 33, 87, 209, 271
    Light, 235, 253
    Love, 51, 63, 75, 315, 321, 327, 333, 339
Thoughts and Conditioned Mind
    Binding Habits, 4, 9, 21, 57, 81, 87, 127, 145 177, 183, 279, 303, 309, 333
    Clever vs. Wise, 9
    Fitting In, 51, 57

REFLECTIONS AND PRACTICES INDEX

II. Nature Helps Us Remember Our True Nature

Animal and Reptile Inspirations
    Coyote, 57
    Deer, 265
    Dog, 63, 139, 209
    Rabbit, 203
    Squirrel, 81
    Turtle, 87

Bird Inspirations
    Geese, 69
    Hummingbird, 75

Home Inspirations
    Bell, 309
    Farmer's Market, 33, 227
    Garden, 127, 321
    Quilt, 321

Human Inspirations
    Ancestors and Elders, 1, 39, 69, 171, 191, 209, 215, 247, 271, 285, 321
    Children, 107, 133, 139, 145
    Childhood Memories, 39, 57, 63, 171, 191, 221, 241, 279, 303
    Plane Ride, 95, 151, 177, 241, 333

Insect Inspirations
    Ant, 45
    Butterfly, 51

Nature Inspirations
    Beach, 107, 259
    Clouds, 241, 285, 333
    Earth, 87, 95, 127, 165, 183, 203, 221, 279, 333
    Field, 203 and 221
    Mist, 315
    Mountain, 45, 285,
    Natural Rhythms, 1, 15, 39, 101, 139, 151, 165, 291, 297, 309
    Rain, 107, 119, 285, 309

REFLECTIONS AND PRACTICES INDEX

River, 27, 51, 87, 95, 101, 107
Sky, 95, 215, 241, 271, 315, 333
Storms, 127, 191, 309, 315, 327
Water, 87, 119
Plant Inspirations
    Daffodil, 9
    Daisy, 253
    Leaf, 15
    Reeds, 27
    Spirals, 151
    Sunflower, 33
    Trees, 15, 21, 39, 171, 191
Sun and Moon Inspirations
    Dawn, 247, 265
    Moon, 69, 159, 197, 215, 235, 259, 271, 309
    Seasons, 15, 133, 151, 165, 197, 203, 209, 221, 227, 247, 291
    Solar Eclipse, 235
    Solstice and Equinox, 15, 203, 291, 297
    Sun, 15, 33, 235, 247, 271, 297

III. **Nature and Poetry Inspire Our Innermost Qualities**
    Abundance, 9, 165, 309
    Acceptance, 51, 57, 191, 241
    Awareness, 75, 133, 177, 221, 247, 291
    Beauty and Radiance, 9, 33, 75, 159, 235, 265, 291
    Clarity, 127, 259, 333
    Delight, 75, 107, 209
    Gentleness, 81, 171, 197
    Giving and Receiving, 171, 203
    Grace, 21, 51, 95, 113, 119, 253
    Gratitude, 51, 75, 227
    Interconnectedness, 45, 75, 107, 139, 145, 183, 221
    Inner Solitude, 303
    Joyfulness, 107, 133, 139, 145, 151, 209, 271

REFLECTIONS AND PRACTICES INDEX

Laughter, 209
Lightness, 15, 45, 75, 133, 235, 253, 285, 291, 315
Listening, 27, 39, 177
Loving, 27, 63, 101, 265, 315, 333
Luminosity, 259, 315, 333
Mountainous, 285
Openness, 221
Peacefulness, 87, 95, 127, 197, 247, 309
Reverence, 197, 215, 227, 265, 279
Spaciousness, 221
Steadfastness, 101, 259, 285, 303
Stillness, 69, 203, 279, 285, 297, 309
Sweetness, 75
Thankfulness, 227
Tranquility, 87
Wholeness, 33 and 227
Wonderment, 9, 21, 159, 215, 271, 279

IV. **Short Practices to Ground Our Wise, Inner Qualities and Attitudes**
Appreciation, 47, 65, 77, 89, 141, 147, 167, 173, 185, 267, 317, 341
Beauty, 161
Gratitude, 223, 287
Joyfulness, 47, 71, 109, 121, 211, 299, 329
Kindness, 223
Letting Go, 17, 23, 41, 97, 109, 121, 173, 223, 249, 261, 273, 305, 311
Releasing, 115, 281, 329
Receiving, 41, 229, 335
Reverence, 11, 47, 77, 217, 293
Smile, 17, 109, 205, 211, 249, 255, 273
Connectivity to the Divine in All
Joy, 59 109, 229, 249, 329

353

REFLECTIONS AND PRACTICES INDEX

Light, 35, 205, 229, 237, 249, 255, 261, 281, 293, 323, 335
Love, 11, 29, 65, 77, 179, 199, 223, 249, 281, 293, 317, 323, 329, 335, 341
Timeless Harmony and Peace, 23, 59, 71, 97, 161, 237, 243, 335
Living Connectivity in All of Life,
    Earth, 29, 129, 135, 229, 299
    Go Outside, 17
    Other Beings, 141
    Space, 83, 135, 217, 299
    Water, 97, 121
Wholeness of Being
    Body, 41, 47, 65, 77, 83, 89, 97, 121, 167, 199, 211, 229, 255, 273, 305, 317, 335, 341
    Breath, 23, 29, 35, 41, 53, 71, 77, 103, 129, 147, 194, 199, 205, 211, 243, 267, 273, 281, 293, 329
    Heart Center, 17, 35, 47, 53, 59, 65, 147, 167, 179, 194, 205, 211, 217, 229, 243, 261, 281, 293, 299, 323, 341
    Senses
        Ears and Sound, 83, 147, 153, 179, 199, 305, 311
        Eyes and Sight, 115, 147, 161, 199, 217, 305, 311
        Hands and Touch, 23, 41, 47, 53, 65, 103, 121, 147, 167, 173, 179, 199, 185, 317

ABOUT THE AUTHOR

Kate Vogt is coeditor of *Mala of the Heart: 108 Sacred Poems* and *Mala of Love: 108 Luminous Poems*, both published by New World Library. She shares wisdom practices that she has honed over two decades through writing, teaching, and mentoring.

Kate's ancestral roots inspire this collection. She grew up in the flatlands of western Kansas, where her family members have been wheat farmers for 100 years. The elders in her community modeled a deep reverence for the earth, and for living a life guided by wisdom.

www.ingramcontent.com/pod-product-compliance
Lightning Source LLC
Chambersburg PA
CBHW042112100526
44587CB00025B/4029